Marriage

and

Family

◆

An Introduction Using MicroCase®

◆

Kevin Demmitt
CLAYTON STATE COLLEGE

Software created by
MicroCase Corporation
Bellevue, Washington

MARRIAGE & FAMILY: An Introduction Using MicroCase is published by MicroCase Corporation.

Editor	David Smetters
Production Supervisor	Jodi B. Gleason
Layout / Electronic Production	Michael Brugman Design
Copy Editors	Judith Abrahms
	Margaret Moore

IBM PC and IBM PC DOS are registered trademarks of International Business Machines, Inc.
ShowCase and **MicroCase** are registered trademarks of MicroCase Corporation.

Printed in the United States of America
1 2 3 4 5 6 7 8 9 10—99 98 97

CONTENTS

Acknowledgments v
Disclaimer of Warranty vi

Introduction 1

Chapters

CHAPTER 1   Regional Variations in Family Structure 3

CHAPTER 2   Singles, Families, and Society...21

CHAPTER 3   Family Values 37

CHAPTER 4   Premarital Sex 51

CHAPTER 5   Mate Selection: Homogamy or Heterogamy 65

CHAPTER 6   Mobile Families and Communities..77

CHAPTER 7   Gender Roles 87

CHAPTER 8   Female Employment, 1920–1990 97

CHAPTER 9   Marital Happiness 109

CHAPTER 10   Marital and Extramarital Sex...119

CHAPTER 11   Fertility and Family Life..131

CHAPTER 12   Childrearing 143

CHAPTER 13   Families and Education: An Introduction to Multiple Regression 153

CHAPTER 14   Divorce Rates 167

CHAPTER 15   The Divorced American 183

CHAPTER 16   Remarriage 193

Codebooks 201

Short Label: NORC 201
Short Label: NSC 201
Short Label: STATES..202
Long Label: NORC 203
Long Label: NSC 208
Long Label: STATES...210

License Agreement..216

ACKNOWLEDGMENTS

It would be impossible to fully recognize everyone who has contributed to the writing of this book. My first exposure to MicroCase was through the materials authored by Rodney Stark at the University of Washington. His leadership in making social research accessible to students has transformed the way I teach and provided the motivation for this book. Many of the introductions to the statistical procedures in this book are based on explanations he has found to be successful with students through the years.

The wide variety of variables used in this book would not be possible without the efforts of the National Opinion Research Center, which directs and administers the U.S. General Social Survey, upon which many of these exercises are based. Thanks must also go to Child Trends, Inc., which maintains and distributes the National Survey of Children for the American Family Data Archive at Sociometrics Corporation.

The actual writing and development of this book was in many ways a team project with MicroCase Corporation. David Smetters' ability to see this text from both the student's and the instructor's perspective was invaluable. Jodi Gleason, the production supervisor, contributed substantially to the final editing of the manuscript and in pulling the many loose ends together. Everyone at MicroCase deserves recognition for putting more time and effort into this final product than one could ever expect of a publisher.

I would also like to acknowledge the contributions of the following individuals who teach marriage and family courses themselves and provided ideas and valuable feedback in the development of this text: Ray Darville at Stephen F. Austin University, Jerry Michel at the University of Memphis, Richard Miller at Missouri Southern State College, Charles O'Conner at Bemidji State University, Leland Robinson at the University of Tennessee-Chattanooga, Ed Sabin at Towson State University, and Roberta Satow at Brooklyn College.

I also wish to acknowledge my friends and colleagues at Clayton State College. Their commitment to innovative and effective teaching is a source of inspiration for trying new ideas in the classroom.

Lastly, I wish to express my gratitude to my wife, Audrey, and my three children, Andrew, Hannah, and Jacob—without whom I would never have started this endeavor. They are the ones who have taught me the value and joy of family life.

Introduction

Welcome to the real world of marriage and family research. There is nothing make-believe about what you will be doing with this Student Version of MicroCase. All of the data are real. In fact, they are some of the best data available to professional researchers, and you will be using some of the same research techniques they employ.

The software is so easy to use that you will learn it without study—just start with the first exercise and follow along. Despite being easy, this software is not a toy. Its computational heart is the same as that of the full MicroCase Analysis System.

◆ GETTING STARTED ◆

This student version of MicroCase requires an IBM PC or fully compatible computer with a VGA (or Super VGA) graphics card, 640K of memory, and 1.44-MB (high density) 3-1/2" disk drive.

To begin, make sure your computer is at the DOS system prompt (which looks something like C:>). Then place the diskette in the A or B drive. If you placed the diskette in the A drive, *type* **A:** and *press <ENTER>*; if you placed the diskette in the B drive, *type* **B:** and *press <ENTER>*. Then *type* **MC** and *press <ENTER>*. It will take about 20 to 30 seconds for the program to load.

Important: The first time you start Student MicroCase, you will be asked to enter your name. It is important to type your name correctly, since it will appear on all printed output. Type your name and *press <ENTER>*. If it is correct, simply *press <ENTER>* in response to the next prompt. (If you wish to correct a mistake, *type* **Y** at the prompt and *press <ENTER>*.) The copyright screen will appear. *Press <ENTER>* to continue.

MicroCase works from two primary menus—one menu is blue, the other is red. When you enter the program and pass beyond the title screen, the blue menu will be on the screen. It looks like this:

```
┌──────────────────────────────────────────────────────────────────────┐
║                   DATA  AND  FILE  MANAGEMENT                          ║
║ ──────────────────────────────────────────────────────────────────    ║
║                                                                        ║
║  S. Switch To STATISTICAL ANALYSIS MENU                                ║
║                                                                        ║
║     DATA MANAGEMENT:                                                   ║
║        A. Define Variables/Recodes      E. Codebook                    ║
║        B. Collapse/Strip Variables      F. Edit Variable Information   ║
║        C. Enter Data from Keyboard      G. Grading Recode              ║
║        D. List or Print Variable Values H. Setup Data Entry            ║
║                                                                        ║
║     FILE MANAGEMENT:                                                   ║
║    * I. Open, Look, Erase or Copy File  M. Move Data between Files     ║
║        J. Create New Data File          N. Merge Files                 ║
║        K. Create Subset File            O. Create Aggregation File     ║
║        L. Import/Export Data            P. Create Statistical Summary  ║
║                                                                        ║
║    *X. EXIT from MicroCase                                             ║
└──────────────────────────────────────────────────────────────────────┘
```

Notice that the highlight is on **I. Open, Look, Erase or Copy File**. This is the only task listed on this menu that is available in this version of the program, and that is why there is an asterisk to the left of the letter I. In order to analyze data, you must open a data file. So, *press* the *<ENTER>* key. The screen now displays the three data files available to you: **NORC**, **NCS**, and **STATES**. To open a file, place the highlight over its name and *press <ENTER>*. You can always move the highlight around by using the arrow keys. Move the highlight to **STATES**. *Press <ENTER>* to open this file; *press <ENTER>* again to return to the menu.

Notice that the highlight is at the top of the screen on **S. Switch To STATISTICAL ANALYSIS MENU**. To switch to the second menu, just *press <ENTER>*. You can always move from one menu to the other by typing S. Now you are on the red menu, which looks like this:

```
                         STATISTICAL ANALYSIS
    ─────────────────────────────────────────────────────────────

    * S. Switch To STATISTICAL ANALYSIS MENU

     BASIC STATISTICAL ANALYSIS:
        *A. Univariate Statistics        *F. Scatterplots
        *B. Tabular Statistics           *G. Correlation
         C. Analysis of Variance          H. Partial Correlation
         D. Covariance Analysis          *I. Regression
        *E. Mapping Variables

     ADVANCED STATISTICAL ANALYSIS:
         J. Regression Models             L. Factor Analysis
         K. Curve Fitting                 M. Logistic Regression
                                          N. Time Series

         Q. Interactive Batch
     *X. EXIT from MicroCase
                                              OPEN FILE: STATES
```

Of these statistical functions, only six are available in this version of the software. Not all six are available at any one time, since several are suitable only for certain kinds of data. For example, mapping and scatterplot functions are useful only with aggregate data such as states, while cross-tabulation is appropriate only for survey data. Thus, what is available on the red screen will depend on which data set you have open. You can tell which functions are available by noting the asterisks to the left of the names. In the exercises that follow, you will be introduced to each of these functions and learn how to use and interpret each.

When you are finished using MicroCase, simply *type* **X** from the main menu, or put the highlight on **EXIT from MicroCase** and *press <ENTER>*. The exit command appears on both the red and blue menus.

If these instructions have left you with a lot of questions, don't worry. Each exercise will carefully lead you through the pertinent parts of the program. There is also a *Quick Guide for MicroCase* located inside the front cover of this book. Refer to this guide if you have questions about basic operations in MicroCase.

◆ CHAPTER 1 ◆

Regional Variations in Family Structure

The family, like all other social institutions, can be viewed through a microscope or a telescope. For example, if I asked you to describe *your* family, you would give me the microscopic view. You would probably describe your parents, siblings, and other relatives, and the experiences you had growing up. However, if I asked you to write an essay on *the* family, you would undoubtedly give me a very different answer. Rather than describing unique individuals, you would focus on social positions, or **statuses**, such as those of mothers, fathers, children, grandparents, husbands, wives, and so on, and the social expectations, or **roles**, attached to each status. The combination of social statuses that make up a family unit are referred to as the **family structure**. In looking at the family from this perspective, we see an institution that is characterized by diversity. In addition to the **nuclear family**, consisting of father, mother, and children, there are single-parent families, families with stepchildren, couples without children, multigenerational families, and a host of other family structures. In this exercise, we will examine the similarities and differences in family structures across the U.S. Along the way, you will learn how to operate the accompanying software and master some basic research techniques.

Does the place where you live have any bearing on whether or not you will get married? Are you more likely to get divorced if you happen to live in the West than if you live in the South or the Midwest? Many people would answer *no* to both of these questions. After all, getting married or divorced is an individual decision—how could the region of the country you live in possibly make a difference? On the other hand, if regions of the country vary with regard to their cultures or economic characteristics, then where you live *could* make a difference. Perhaps people who live in one place share family-related values that differ from those of people who live elsewhere. Maybe the availability of good jobs or schools, or a number of other environmental factors that vary geographically, have an impact on the familial decisions people make. If this is the case, we would in fact expect to find regional differences in family structures.

Let's use the data we have available to see whether family structures are the same or different from one region of the U.S. to another. If you have not already done so, start MicroCase according to the instructions in the *Introduction*. With the highlight on **I. Open, Look, Erase or Copy File**, *press <ENTER>*. The diskette contains three files, or data sets: **NORC**, **NSC**, and **STATES**. Using the **arrow** keys to move the highlight, place it on **STATES** and *press <ENTER>*. Much of the data used in this exercise was taken from the 1990 U.S. Census. The screen will tell you that this data file is based on the 50 states and includes 96 variables. *Press <ENTER>* to return to the menu. The highlight is now at the top of the screen on the line reading **Switch To STATISTICAL ANALYSIS MENU**. *Press <ENTER>* to switch to that menu. Place the highlight on **E. Mapping Variables** and *press <ENTER>*. Now you are asked for the name or number of the variable you wish to map.

A **variable** is anything that varies among the objects being examined. For example, all states have rules as to what constitutes a marriage. Therefore, states that have legally defined marriages *is not* a variable because all states have legally defined marriages. However, the number of legally recognized marriages in each state does vary. Thus, the *percentage* of the population in each state that is married *is* a variable. States also differ in the proportions of their populations who remain single, have children, go camping, go to church, are wealthy, or drop out of school—all of these could be variables. Or, if we are examining individuals rather than states, all traits and characteristics in which people differ—height, weight, political opinions, hobbies, or education, for example—are variables.

Let's take a look at the percentage of households occupied by married couples to see if there are regional variations. Returning to your computer, *type* **28** or **COUPLES** and *press <ENTER>*. (In fact, you need only type enough of the variable name to make it unique and the computer will fill in the rest. So in this case you could have simply typed COU and pressed <ENTER>.)

A map of the U.S. appears on your screen. It shows the percentage of households occupied by married couples according to the 1990 U.S. Census. The darker a state looks, the greater its percentage of married couples. The map on your screen will look like this:

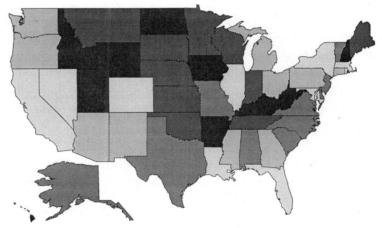

1990: Percent of Households with Married Couples

Indeed, there are some distinct regional variations. The distribution of the married population in the U.S. is not random. Most of the states with the highest couple rates are clustered in the central portion of the U.S. The states with the lowest couple rates tend to be found along the coasts.

Let's look to see which state scored the highest. *Type* **N** (for Name). The name Utah appears on the screen and an arrow points to that state. At the bottom left corner of the screen we see the state's name and that 65.75 percent of its households were occupied by married couples in 1990. *Press* the **down arrow** key to move to the next highest state. Now the screen shows us that Idaho ranked second highest, with about 63 percent. If you keep pressing the **down arrow** key, you will be able to see the percentage for each state as its name appears. However, if you want to see all 50 states ranked from high to low on the married-couples rate, simply *type* **D** (for Distribution). Here we see that six of the ten states with the most married couples are located in the north central U.S. New York is in last place, with 51.1 percent. Nevada ranks second from the bottom, with around 52 percent. If you *type* **A** (for Area map), you will return to the map.

The basic task of social science is to *explain variation*. We do this by trying to *discover connections among variables*. Now that we have seen that the proportion of married couples varies by region in this country, the next step is to try to explain *why* there are fewer married couples outside of America's heartland. Is it because people in other parts of the country are less likely to marry? Or could it be that the likelihood of getting married is the same everywhere, but that couples in some parts of the country are more likely to be separated or divorced? Either of these factors, singleness or divorce, could affect the percentage of married couples. To see whether one or both of these factors influence the married-couples rate, we need to see where the greatest percentage of single and divorced persons is located.

Press <ENTER>. You are asked for the name or number of the next variable you wish to map. This time, *type* **25** or %**SINGLE** and *press <ENTER>*. This map will appear:

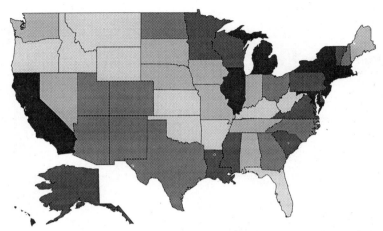

1990: Percent of Persons 15 and Over Who Have Never Been Married

Here we see the percentage of the population in each state who are aged 15 and older and have never married. This map is nearly a reverse image of the map for married couples. The coastal states are generally darker than the central states, which means they have a greater percentage of single adults. Now let's see which state has the greatest percentage of adults who have never been married. *Type* **N** (for Name). The name Massachusetts appears on the screen, with a percentage of 65.8. *Press* the **down arrow** key. New York, which had the lowest couples rate, has the second highest percentage of adults who have never been married. *Type* **D** (for Distribution) to look at the entire range of 50 states. Arkansas has the lowest percentage of adults who have never married (41.7 percent), followed by Oklahoma (42.2 percent) and Idaho (42.6 percent). Many of the states that had a high percentage of married couples are clustered among the states that have a low percentage of unmarried adults.

We will look at the divorced population shortly, but first let's explore this distribution of the singles population a little further. We still don't know *why* there are more singles along the coasts and fewer singles in the central states. One explanation for the larger number of singles in some states than in others would be an imbalance in the gender ratio of available partners. In other words, there may be an overabundance of single men or single women along the coasts. To see whether that is the case, we need to compare the map of single males with the map of single females.

Press <ENTER> twice to get ready to look at a different map. This time, we will use another technique to select the variable. When you are asked for the name or number of the variable to map, *press* **F3**.

A window opens, as shown here:

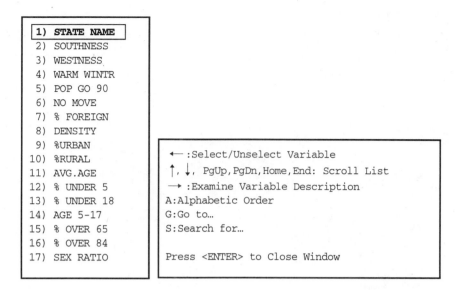

```
 ┌─────────────────┐
 │ 1) STATE NAME   │
 │ 2) SOUTHNESS    │
 │ 3) WESTNESS     │
 │ 4) WARM WINTR   │
 │ 5) POP GO 90    │
 │ 6) NO MOVE      │
 │ 7) % FOREIGN    │
 │ 8) DENSITY      │      ┌──────────────────────────────────────┐
 │ 9) %URBAN       │      │ ← :Select/Unselect Variable          │
 │10) %RURAL       │      │ ↑,↓, PgUp,PgDn,Home,End: Scroll List │
 │11) AVG.AGE      │      │ → :Examine Variable Description       │
 │12) % UNDER 5    │      │ A:Alphabetic Order                    │
 │13) % UNDER 18   │      │ G:Go to…                              │
 │14) AGE 5-17     │      │ S:Search for…                         │
 │15) % OVER 65    │      │                                       │
 │16) % OVER 84    │      │ Press <ENTER> to Close Window         │
 │17) SEX RATIO    │      └──────────────────────────────────────┘
 └─────────────────┘
```

This window shows you the name and number of every variable in any given MicroCase data file. Use the **up** and **down arrow** keys to place the highlight on a given variable. The **page up** and **page down** keys will let you move more rapidly up and down the list. The **end** key will take you to the bottom of the list. The **home** key will take you back to the beginning of the list.

Now place the highlight on the variable **26) %SINGLE M** and *press* the **right arrow** key. An additional window opens, as shown below.

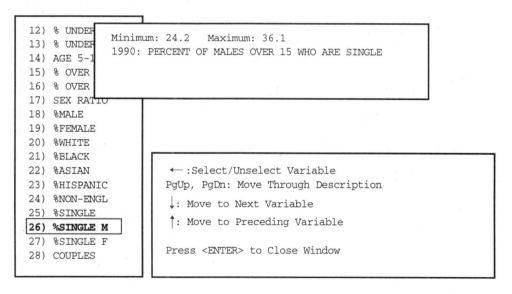

```
 ┌────────────┌──────────────────────────────────────────────────┐
 │12) % UNDEF │  Minimum: 24.2   Maximum: 36.1                    │
 │13) % UNDEF │  1990: PERCENT OF MALES OVER 15 WHO ARE SINGLE    │
 │14) AGE 5-1 │                                                   │
 │15) % OVER  │                                                   │
 │16) % OVER  │                                                   │
 │17) SEX RATIO                                                   │
 │18) %MALE   └──────────────────────────────────────────────────┘
 │19) %FEMALE
 │20) %WHITE
 │21) %BLACK
 │22) %ASIAN      ┌──────────────────────────────────────────────┐
 │23) %HISPANIC   │ ← :Select/Unselect Variable                  │
 │24) %NON-ENGL   │ PgUp, PgDn: Move Through Description          │
 │25) %SINGLE     │ ↓: Move to Next Variable                     │
 │26) %SINGLE M   │ ↑: Move to Preceding Variable                │
 │27) %SINGLE F   │                                              │
 │28) COUPLES     │ Press <ENTER> to Close Window                │
 └────────────    └──────────────────────────────────────────────┘
```

This window shows you a full description of the variable **26) %SINGLE M**, which lets you know that this variable consists of the percentage of the population in each state that is single and male. To close this window, *press <ENTER>*. To select this variable for analysis, *press* the **left arrow** key. Notice that a mark appears next to the name of the variable. This indicates that you have selected the variable. *Press <ENTER>.*

Marriage and Family

The map representing the distribution of single males across the country appears on the screen. It is nearly identical to the preceding map. *Press* **C** (for Compare) and the map shrinks to half-size and moves to the top of the screen. The screen asks for the name or number of the variable for comparison. *Type* **27** or **%SINGLE F** and *press* *<ENTER>*. The map showing the distribution of the single female population appears on the bottom half of the screen.

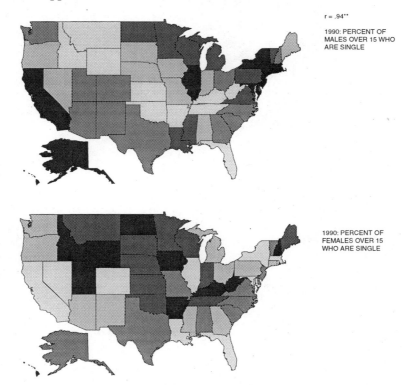

r = .94**

1990: PERCENT OF
MALES OVER 15 WHO
ARE SINGLE

1990: PERCENT OF
FEMALES OVER 15
WHO ARE SINGLE

The two maps look surprisingly similar. The highest concentrations of single males are located in the same regions as the highest concentrations of single females. Both single men and single women are most likely to live in New England or along the West Coast. The lower married-couples rates in these areas cannot be attributed to a lack of available marriage partners.

So a social researcher wishing to explore this topic further might ask, "*Why* are there fewer single people in America's heartland?" Are the young people raised there really more likely to get married? Or have most of the single adults simply relocated to the coastal states? Although we will not be able to answer these questions definitively, you may come up with some possible explanations by the time you finish this exercise. *Press* *<ENTER>* several times until you return to the initial prompt requesting you to select a variable to be mapped.

Divorce is another factor that can decrease the couple rate. To examine this variable, *type* **32** or **%DIVORCED** and *press* *<ENTER>*.

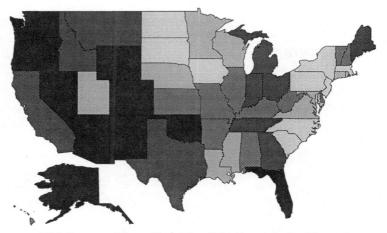

1990: Percent of Those 15 and Over Who Currently Are Divorced

This map presents a snapshot of persons who are currently divorced (those who have divorced and remarried were represented in the map of married couples). Whereas singleness is a bicoastal phenomenon, divorce is skewed more to the west. Nine of the ten states with the highest percentage of divorced residents are located west of the Mississippi River. *Type* **D** to see the distribution. Nevada has the highest rate of residents who are currently divorced, with 14.4 percent, followed by Alaska (11.1 percent) and Oregon (10.8 percent). North Dakota (6 percent) has the lowest rate of divorced residents. *Press <ENTER>* to return to the map.

Type **S** (for Spot). The map changes and a series of spots (or dots) of different sizes and colors appear, one dot for each state. Now, in addition to color differences to indicate which states are higher or lower, the spot for each state is proportional to the value of the variable being mapped. Thus Nevada has the largest spot and North Dakota has the smallest. Many people find the spots much easier to interpret than when only color cues are used.

You also can use spot maps for comparison; each comparison map will also be a spot map. *Type* **C** (for Compare). You are asked for the name or number of the variable for comparison. *Type* **28** or **COUPLES** and *press <ENTER>*.

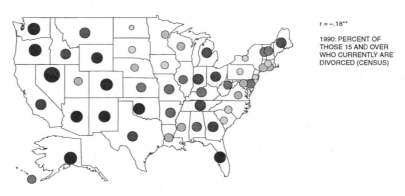

r = −.18**

1990: PERCENT OF
THOSE 15 AND OVER
WHO CURRENTLY ARE
DIVORCED (CENSUS)

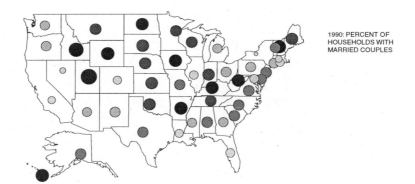

1990: PERCENT OF
HOUSEHOLDS WITH
MARRIED COUPLES

As expected, the map showing where married couples are concentrated is not very similar to the map showing where currently divorced individuals reside. With the exception of Florida, the ten states with the highest rates are all located west of the Mississippi River. The north central states are among those with the fewest divorced residents. So not only are there fewer singles living in America's heartland, there are fewer divorced individuals living there as well. Lower rates of both singleness and divorce help to explain the high percentage of married couples in the central states. People who live there are more likely to marry and also are more likely to stay married.

One other family structure to examine is that of female-headed households. *Press <ENTER>* three times to clear the screen for a new map. When asked for the name or number of a variable, *type* **36** or **%FEM.HEAD** and *press <ENTER>*.

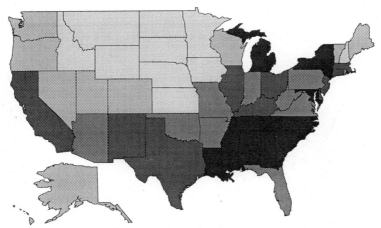

1990: Percent of Households That Are Female-headed, No Spouse Present

The highest concentration of female-headed households is in the Southeast. *Type* **N** and you see that 15.57 percent of the households in Mississippi are headed by single women. *Press* the **down arrow** key. Louisiana has the second highest rate, with 15.34 percent. *Type* **D** (for Distribution). The two states with the next highest percentages of female-headed households (South Carolina and Georgia) are also in the Southeast. North Dakota has the fewest female-headed households, with 7.11 percent.

Is the large number of female-headed families in the South a result of divorce or of premarital pregnancies? *Press <ENTER>* to return to the map and *press* **C** (for Compare). When you are asked for the name or number of a variable for comparison, *type* **34** or **%F.DIVORCE** and *press <ENTER>*.

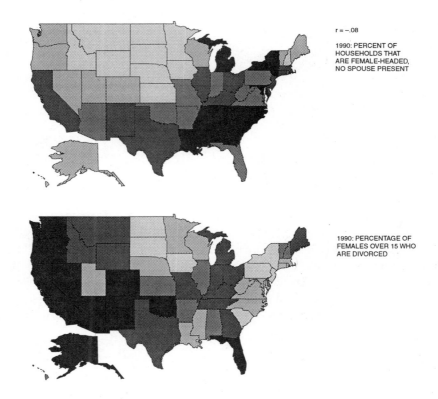

r = –.08

1990: PERCENT OF
HOUSEHOLDS THAT
ARE FEMALE-HEADED,
NO SPOUSE PRESENT

1990: PERCENTAGE OF
FEMALES OVER 15 WHO
ARE DIVORCED

These two maps are not very similar. There are more divorced women on the West Coast than there are in the South. *Press <ENTER>*. You are again asked for the name or number of a variable to use for comparison. This time, *type* **42** or **TEEN MOMS** and *press <ENTER>*.

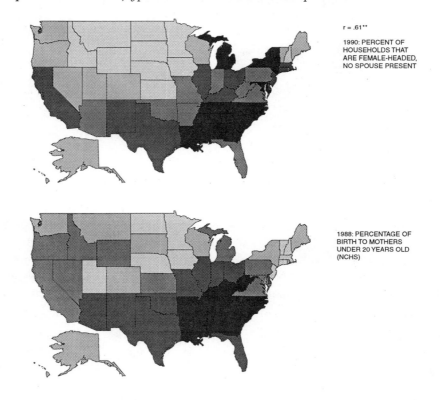

r = .61**

1990: PERCENT OF
HOUSEHOLDS THAT
ARE FEMALE-HEADED,
NO SPOUSE PRESENT

1988: PERCENTAGE OF
BIRTH TO MOTHERS
UNDER 20 YEARS OLD
(NCHS)

Marriage and Family

These two maps are quite similar. Because teenage mothers are less likely than older women who have children to be married, it would appear that the high number of female-headed families in the South results from premarital pregnancies rather than from divorce.

What we have seen thus far demonstrates that family structures are not randomly distributed throughout the country. Although nearly half of the adults living in every state are married, there are some distinct trends. The states along the coasts have more singles. There are more divorced persons in the West. The South has a higher percentage of female-headed households. The north central states have the highest percentage of married couples. These are all trends that you would miss if you looked only at isolated individuals.

Although most people consider getting married or divorced (or a similar familial decision) to be an individual choice, the trends we have observed tell us that these decisions are influenced by factors beyond the individual. The larger sociocultural environment does play a role in the decisions people make.

This exercise has been primarily descriptive and has focused almost exclusively on family structures. In the exercises that follow, you will have the opportunity to examine maps of family structures and compare them with maps of other social phenomena.

NAME: _____

COURSE: _____

DATE: _____

1. Open the **STATES** data file and select the mapping function. Map variable **35** or **%MALE.HEAD**.

    Write in the caption of the map: _____

    _____

    Press **D** (for Distribution).

    List the five highest states: 1. _____

                                     2. _____

                                     3. _____

                                     4. _____

                                     5. _____

    In general, which region of the U.S. (e.g., Northeast, Midwest, Plains, South, Southwest, West) has the highest rate of male-headed homes?   _____

    List the five lowest states: 46. _____

                                    47. _____

                                    48. _____

                                    49. _____

                                    50. _____

    In general, which region of the U.S. has the lowest rate of male-headed homes?   _____

2. Create a new map of **36** or **%FEM.HEAD**.

    Write in the caption of the map: _____

    _____

    Press **D** (for Distribution).

WORKSHEET

List the five highest states:

1. _____

2. _____

3. _____

4. _____

5. _____

In general, which region of the U.S. has the highest rate of female-headed homes?

_____

List the five lowest states:

46. _____

47. _____

48. _____

49. _____

50. _____

In general, which region of the U.S. has the lowest rate of female-headed homes?

_____

In a few sentences, summarize the results you found for the first two questions.

3. Now map variable **15 or % OVER 65**.

Write in the caption of the map: _____

_____

Press **D** (for Distribution).

List the three highest states:

1. _____

2. _____

3. _____

List the three lowest states:　　48. _____

49. _____

50. _____

Return to the full map and select the Compare function. Use **38** or **HHOLD SIZE** as the second map.

Write in the caption of the map: _____

_____

Would you say these maps are (circle one):

Very Similar

Somewhat Similar

Not Very Similar

Press <ENTER> once. Use **32** or *%***DIVORCED** as the second map.

Write in the caption of the map: _____

_____

Would you say these maps are (circle one):

Very Similar

Somewhat Similar

Not Very Similar

Using these results, what can you say about the regions of the country that have high proportions of older people in regard to divorce and household size?

4.　Return to the beginning of the task and map variable **44** or **ABORTION**.

Write in the caption of the map: _____

_____

Press **D** (for Distribution).

List the three highest states:

1. _____

2. _____

3. _____

List the three lowest states:

48. _____

49. _____

50. _____

Return to the map and *press* **S** (for Spot map). Now use the Compare function and select **27** or **%SINGLE F** as the second map.

Write in the caption of the map: _____

_____

Would you say these maps are (circle one):

Very Similar

Somewhat Similar

Not Very Similar

Press <ENTER> once. Use **53** or % **COLLEGE** as the second map.

Write in the caption of the map: _____

_____

Would you say these maps are (circle one):

Very Similar

Somewhat Similar

Not Very Similar

Using these results, suggest why some states may have more abortions than others. Explain.

5. Return to the beginning of the task and map variable **46** or **%POOR.FAM**.

Write in the caption of the map: _____

_____

Press **D** (for Distribution).

List the three highest states: 1. _____

2. _____

3. _____

List the three lowest states: 48. _____

49. _____

50. _____

Return to the map and *press* **C** (for Compare). Select **36** or **%FEM.HEAD** as the second map.

Would you say these maps are (circle one):   Very Similar

Somewhat Similar

Not Very Similar

Press <*ENTER*>. Use **35** or **%MALE.HEAD** as the second map.

Would you say these maps are (circle one):   Very Similar

Somewhat Similar

Not Very Similar

Were the results of these comparisons what you expected? Explain.

6.   Now you can select your own maps to compare. Choose a variable you would like to map and type its name or number. (Remember, you can also use **F3** to select variables, or you can consult the list of variables in the back of your book and type in the name or number of the variable you wish to select.)

Which variable did you select? _____

Write in the caption of the map: _____

_____

Press **P** to print this map. (**Note:** If your computer is not connected to a printer or if you have been instructed not to use the printer, skip these printing instructions.) When you print a graphic (e.g., a map or bar graph), the program will ask whether you are using a laser, dot matrix, or Bubblejet printer. Once you make the appropriate choice, MicroCase will print a copy of this map. It may take some time to print a graphic such as this. Your name and the date will be printed along with the map. Attach a copy of the map to this exercise.

Press **D** (for Distribution).

List the three highest states: 1. _____

                                            2. _____

                                            3. _____

List the three lowest states: 48. _____

                                            49. _____

                                            50. _____

Press *<ENTER>* twice to clear the screen for another map. Select a variable to map that you believe will be similar to your previous map.

Which variable did you select? _____

Why do you think this map will be similar to your first map?

Write in the caption of the map: _____

_____

Press **P** to print this map. Attach a copy of the map to this exercise.

Were the results of these comparisons what you expected when you selected these variables? Explain.

◆ CHAPTER 2 ◆
Singles, Families, and Society

Although family life is something most Americans believe is very private, the distinct social patterns we observed in Exercise 1 remind us that the family is a part of a larger social landscape. By studying the social environment surrounding the family, we can gain a better understanding of how the family is related to society at large. To demonstrate how even very private acts have broader social implications, we will begin this exercise by examining some trends associated with sexuality. Then we will go on to look at how the family is related to other social phenomena, such as crime and poverty.

Let's revisit the distribution of never-married individuals in the U.S. and consider the effects of having a large single adult population. If you have not already done so, start MicroCase according to the instructions given in the *Introduction*. Open the **STATES** data file and go to the **STATIS-TICAL ANALYSIS MENU**. Place the highlight on **E. Mapping Variables** and *press <ENTER>*. Now you are asked for the name or number of the variable you wish to map. *Type* **25** or %**SINGLE** and *press <ENTER>*. *Press* **S** (for Spot map).

1990: Percent of Persons 15 and Over Who Have Never Been Married

As you may recall, the unmarried population is distributed primarily in the urban coastal states. *Press* **D** (for Distribution) and you can review the states that had the highest and lowest proportions of singles.

What are some of the social trends you might find in a region populated by more single adults? For example, it would seem probable that single adults are more likely than those who are married to have had multiple sex partners in recent years. So, do states that have large singles populations also have more deaths resulting from AIDS?

Press **S** to return to the spot map and then *press* **C** (for Compare). When you are asked for the name or number of the variable for comparison, *type* **73** or **AIDS** and *press <ENTER>*. This map shows the number of deaths attributed to AIDS per 100,000 residents in each state.

r = .62**

1990: PERCENT OF
PERSONS 15 AND
OVER WHO HAVE NEVER
BEEN MARRIED (CENSUS)

1991: TOTAL NUMBER OF
AIDS DEATHS PER 100,000
THROUGH 1991 (HEALTH,
1992)

Notice how very much alike these two maps are. Both have higher rates along each coast. The states with smaller dots and lighter shading are situated more in the center than in any other part of the country.

When you did Exercise 1, you undoubtedly found it easy to see when two maps were as similar as the two above. But as you examined the maps that were less similar, you may have found it more difficult to say how similar they were.

It also becomes more difficult to say how similar any two maps are when the maps are very complex. For example, it would be much harder to compare two maps based on the 3,142 counties of the U.S. than two maps based on the 50 states. The same is true of attempts to compare lists. It is not too hard to compare lists of the 50 states, but it would be much more difficult to compare longer lists. Thus, it was a considerable achievement when, in the 1890s, an Englishman named Karl Pearson discovered an extremely simple method for comparing maps or lists.

To see Pearson's method, we can draw a horizontal line across the bottom of a sheet of paper. We will let this line represent the number of AIDS cases. At the left end of this line, we will write 2.0, which indicates the state with the fewest AIDS-related deaths per 100,000 population: South Dakota. At the right end of the line, we will place the number 152.4 to represent New York, the state with the most AIDS-related deaths per 100,000 population.

2.0   152.4

Now we can draw a vertical line up the left side of the paper. This line will represent the proportion of single adults in a given state. At the bottom of this line, we will write 41.7 to represent Arkansas, the state with the lowest rate. At the top, we will write 65.8 to represent Massachusetts, the state with the highest rate.

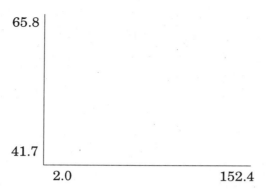

Now that we have a line with an appropriate scale to represent each map, the next thing we need to do is look at the distribution for each map to obtain the value for each state and then locate it on each side according to its score. Let's start with New York. Since it has the most deaths per 100,000 attributed to AIDS, we can easily find its place on the horizontal axis above. Make a small mark at 152.4 to locate New York. Next, New York has the second highest singles rate, so estimate where a rate of 64.7 is located on the vertical line. Knowing where New York is on each line representing each map, we can draw a vertical line up from its position on the line for AIDS deaths and we can draw a horizontal line out from its position on the line for single adults. Where these two lines meet (or cross), we can make a dot. This dot represents the combined map location of New York.

Now let's locate New Jersey. Its AIDS-death rate is 99.1 per 100,000 residents, so we can make a mark on the horizontal line at that spot. Its married-couples rate is 58.7, so we can mark that point on the vertical line. The point where these two lines meet is the combined map location for New Jersey.

When we have followed this procedure for each state, we will have 50 dots located within the space defined by the vertical and horizontal lines representing the two maps. What we have done is create a **scatterplot**. Fortunately, you don't have to go to all this trouble. MicroCase will do it for you. Return to the red statistical analysis screen by *pressing <ENTER>* several times and select **F. Scatterplots**. When you are asked for the name or number of the dependent variable, *type* **25** or **%SINGLE** and *press <ENTER>*. You are asked for the name or number of the independent variable. *Type* **73** or **AIDS** and *press <ENTER>* twice. This screen will appear:

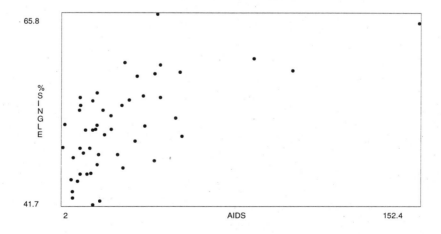

Each of these dots represents a state. *Press* **S** (for Show case), then *type* **OHIO** and *press* *<ENTER>*. Do you see the dot that is flashing on the screen? That dot represents Ohio's combined position on the two maps. *Press <ENTER>* to cause the dot to stop flashing. You can examine the dot for each state in this way. *Press <ENTER>* again. If you have forgotten precisely what either of the two maps represents, you can examine their long labels by *pressing* **X** for the horizontal map and **Y** for the vertical map. If you select either of these options, you will need to *press* *<ENTER>* to clear the window.

Once Pearson had created a scatterplot, his next step was to calculate what he called the *regression line*. To see this line, simply *press* **L** (for regression Line). This line represents the best effort to draw a straight line that connects all the dots. It is unnecessary for you to know how to calculate the location of the regression line because the program does it for you. But if you would like to see how the regression line would look if all the dots were located along a straight line, all you need to do is examine the scatterplot for identical maps. So if you create a scatterplot using **25** or **%SINGLE** for both the dependent and independent variables, you will be comparing identical maps and the dots representing states will all be on the regression line like a straight string of beads.

However, since the maps for AIDS and singles are only very similar, but not identical, most of the dots are scattered near, but not on, the regression line. Pearson's method for calculating how similar any two maps or lists are becomes very easy once the regression line has been drawn. What it amounts to is measuring the distance out from the regression line to every dot. To do this, simply *press* **R** (for Residual). See all the little lines. If you added them all together, you would have the sum of the deviations of the dots from the regression line. The smaller this sum, the more similar are the two maps. For example, when the maps are identical and all the dots are on the regression line, the sum of the deviations is zero.

To make it simple to interpret results, Pearson invented a procedure to convert the sums into a number he called the **correlation coefficient**. The correlation coefficient varies from 0.0 to 1.0. When the maps are identical, the correlation coefficient will be 1.0. When the maps are completely different, the correlation coefficient will be 0.0. Thus, the closer the correlation coefficient is to 1.0, the more similar the two maps or lists are. Pearson used the letter **r** as the symbol for his correlation coefficient. Look at the lower left-hand corner of the screen and you will see **r = 0.624**. This indicates that the maps are similar. There are no steadfast rules for interpreting the strength of a correlation coefficient (r), but as a general guideline, the following rule of thumb can be used with the STATES data file:

.70 or higher	Very strong relationship
.40 to .69	Strong relationship
.30 to .39	Moderate relationship
.20 to .29	Weak relationship
below .20	No or negligible relationship

To the right of the correlation coefficient, you will find the value for **statistical significance**—the odds that the correlation coefficient is a chance finding. It indicates that **Prob. = 0.000**. The probability value is a proportion and, hence, has a range between 0 and 1.0. Simply put, if the value equals .04, that means there are 4 chances out of 100 that the correlation coefficient obtained is a fluke—a chance finding. Social scientists have established a rule for statistical significance as well, but this one is firmer. When the probability value is above .05 (that is, between .05 and 1.00), the correlation coefficient that was found is *not* considered to be statistically significant. If the probability value is below .05 (that is, between .05 and .00), then the correlation coefficient can be considered statistically significant. In this case, the probability equals 0.00, so the correlation is highly significant. It is important to not confuse the concept of correlation with statistical significance. If these concepts are not clear in your mind, try rereading the previous two paragraphs.

Also, keep in mind that correlation and causation are *not* the same thing. It is true that without correlation there can be no causation. Thus, the singles rate cannot be considered a contributing factor in the spread of AIDS *if* there is no correlation between the two variables. But correlations often occur between two variables without one's causing the other. For example, in any grade school you would find a very high correlation between children's height and their reading ability. This correlation occurs because both height and reading ability reflect age—the taller kids are older and the older kids read better. The positive correlation between the singles rate and the AIDS rate may signify a cause-and-effect relationship. However, we cannot rule out the possibility that this positive correlation may actually reflect the trend for more singles to be living in urban areas, where drug use may also contribute to the spread of AIDS.

AIDS is not only spread through sexual contact; it can also be spread by the use of contaminated needles for injecting drugs. Let's see if we can use a scatterplot to demonstrate the connection between illegal drugs and AIDS deaths.

Press <ENTER> twice. When you are prompted for the name of the dependent variable, *type* **73** or **AIDS** and *press <ENTER>*. You are asked for the name or number of the independent variable. *Type* **66** or **COKE USERS** and *press <ENTER>* twice. Although other drugs are more closely associated with using needles, the use of cocaine may be used as a general indicator of illegal drug use.

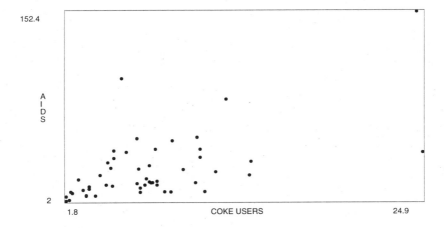

As you may have expected, this scatterplot illustrating the relationship between AIDS deaths and cocaine use is quite similar to the previous one using the percentages of singles. *Press* **L** to see the regression line. The higher the percentage of cocaine users, the greater the rate of AIDS-related deaths (r = 0.588). Notice that the regression line slants upward from left to right, like it did in the previous example. That is another visual cue that there is a strong, positive relationship between the two variables being compared. So, in these examples, both a large single population and a large drug-using population are associated with increased numbers of deaths resulting from AIDS.

Does this mean that there will be fewer AIDS-related deaths in states that have more married couples? *Press <ENTER>*. When you are prompted for the name of the dependent variable, *type*

73 or **AIDS** and *press <ENTER>*. You are asked for the name or number of the independent variable. *Type* **28** or **COUPLES** and *press <ENTER>* twice. Here is how the scatterplot will look:

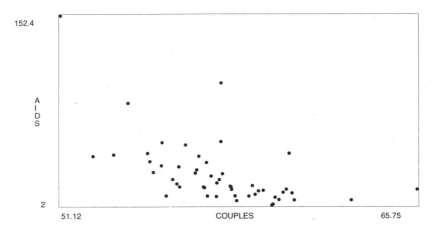

Press **L** to see the regression line. At the bottom of the screen we see that the correlation is –0.581. This is a negative correlation. We can tell that in two ways. First, there is a minus sign preceding the correlation coefficient. Second, the regression line slopes downward from left to right, showing that as the number of households with married couples rises, the rate of AIDS deaths decreases. The positive or negative sign signifies only the direction of the relationship—whether the two variables move in the same direction or in the opposite direction. In other words, a negative correlation of 0.581 is just as strong as a positive correlation of 0.581.

Let's look at another variable that we might expect to be related to the proportion of single males. *Press <ENTER>*. When you are prompted for the name of the dependent variable, *type* **83** or **PLAYBOY** and *press <ENTER>*. You are asked for the name or number of the independent variable. *Type* **26** or **%SINGLE M** and *press <ENTER>* twice. This scatterplot will appear on your screen:

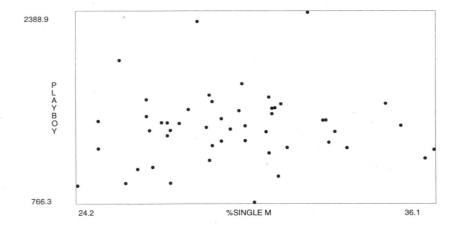

Do areas with more single males have more subscribers to *Playboy* magazine? No. The relationship between these variables is essentially random. The dots are scattered all over the screen. *Press* **L** (for regression Line). The regression line has no slope and simply crosses the screen from left to right. The correlation coefficient is a minuscule 0.069, and Prob. = 0.31—which is well above the .05 value we need for statistical significance.

Perhaps marital status is less important than gender itself in explaining the distribution of *Playboy* magazine subscribers. *Press <ENTER>*. When you are prompted for the name of the dependent variable, *type* **83** or **PLAYBOY** and *press <ENTER>*. You are asked for the name or number of the independent variable. *Type* **18** or **%MALE** and *press <ENTER>* twice. When the scatterplot appears, *press* **L**. This scatterplot will appear on your screen:

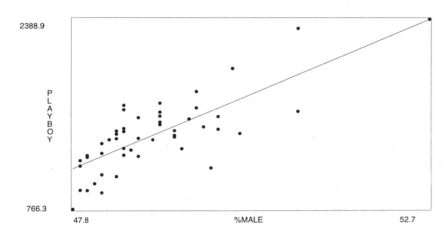

There is clearly a relationship here, and it is positive (r = 0.773). The larger the percentage of the population that is male, the greater the proportion of *Playboy* subscribers. Does this mean that as many married men as single men, or even more, subscribe to *Playboy* magazine? Not necessarily. We cannot make assumptions about individuals when we are using state-level data. These data do not indicate whether it is those who are married or single, or both, who are subscribing to *Playboy* in these states that are predominantly male. But we can say this is one trend that has more to do with the gender of the population than with family structure.

Another reason to be careful about claiming cause-and-effect relationships is that correlations do not indicate which variable occurred first. To illustrate, let's take a look at the relationship between violent crime and female-headed families. *Press <ENTER>* to clear the screen for a new scatterplot. This time, we will select the variables using the **F3** key. When you are asked for the name or number of the dependent variable, *press* **F3**. Use the **page down** and **down arrow** keys to move the highlight to **68) V.CRIME** and *press* the **left arrow** key to select the variable. Move the highlight to **36) %FEM.HEAD**. *Press* the **right arrow** key. The window tells us this variable represents the percentage of families headed by females with no adult males present. *Press* the **left arrow** key to select the variable. *Press <ENTER>* several times until the scatterplot appears. *Press* **L** (for regression Line).

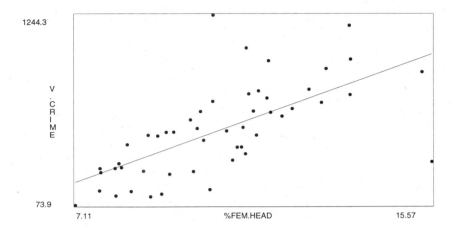

Here you see a positive correlation of 0.659. However, this does not tell us which came first—the violent crime or the prevalence of single-female-parent families. One could argue that the absence of adult males in female-headed households results in more violent crimes because there is less supervision and there are fewer positive male role models. Or one could just as reasonably argue that violence increases the divorce rate and decreases the pool of desirable males, both of which would increase the number of female-headed households. Of course, it could also be that violent crime and female-headed households are simply facets of a common underlying cause—that both are part of contemporary urban life.

Remember that correlation does not necessarily demonstrate causation; variables may be highly correlated without one having caused the other. Nevertheless, social scientists examine correlations primarily to test hypotheses that propose cause-and-effect relationships. To more fully capture this aspect of research, it is helpful to distinguish between **independent** and **dependent variables**. If we think something is the cause of something else, we say that *the cause is the independent variable* and that the *consequence (or the thing that is being caused) is the dependent variable*. To help you remember the difference, think that variables being caused are dependent on the causal variable, whereas causal variables are not dependent, but independent. That is why the scatterplot screen gives you the option of identifying one variable as dependent and the other as independent.

Although the scatterplot was a brilliant invention, and is still essential for analyzing aggregate data, the correlation coefficient can be computed directly. To explore this, *press <ENTER>* several times to return to the main menu and select **G. Correlation**. When you are asked for the name or number of variable 1, *type* **36** or **%FEM.HEAD** and *press <ENTER>*. Use **35** or **%MALE.HEAD** as the second variable, **66** or **COKE USERS** as the third, and **69** or **RAPE** as the fourth, and then *press <ENTER>* twice. These results will appear:

	36) %FEM.HEAD	35) %MALE.HEAD	66) COKE USERS	69) RAPE
36) %FEM.HEAD	—	0.306*	0.248*	0.307*
35) %MALE.HEAD	0.306*	—	0.501**	0.384**
66) COKE USERS	0.248*	0.501**	—	0.196
69) RAPE	0.307*	0.384**	0.196	—

You can discover the correlation between any two variables in either of two ways. First, find one of the two variables in the horizontal list across the top of the screen. Then look down that column until you come to the second variable, as shown in the vertical list to the left of the screen. Thus, you will see that the correlation between the percentage of male-headed homes and cocaine use is 0.501. You can do it the other way, too, looking for one variable at the left and then looking for the other across the top. When a variable is correlated with itself, the result is always a perfect 1.000. All correlations that meet the 0.05 level of statistical significance are indicated by one asterisk; two asterisks indicate significance above the 0.01 level. With regard to the indicators of urban social problems, we see that male-headed homes and female-headed households are similarly correlated with the incidence of rape. However, cocaine use is more prevalent around male-headed households than around female-headed homes. This difference may be related to the high economic cost of supporting cocaine use and the relative incomes of men and women.

In the correlations we have analyzed in this exercise, it is often difficult to say whether family structure is the *cause* or the *effect* of social problems and trends. Social researchers themselves differ on this point. Some believe that social problems such as drug abuse or crime result from the breakdown of the family. Others believe that the breakdown of the family is actually a consequence of broader social problems, such as poverty or discrimination.

In the exercises that follow, you will have the opportunity to look at the ways the family structure is related to some social trends. Feel free to decide for yourself which you believe is the cause and which you think is the effect of each trend.

Your turn.

EXERCISE
2

1. Open the **STATES** data file and select the scatterplot function. Create the following scatterplot:

    Dependent variable: **57** or **MATH SCORE**

    Independent variable: **28** or **COUPLES**

    Write down the long label for **57** or **MATH SCORE** (*press* **Y** to see it):

    _____

    _____

    What is the correlation coefficient?   **r** = _____

    Is this a positive or a negative correlation? (circle one)   Positive   Negative

    Create the following scatterplot:

    Dependent variable: **52** or **DROPOUTS**

    Independent variable: **28** or **COUPLES**

    Write down the long label for **52** or **DROPOUTS** (*press* **Y** to see it):

    _____

    _____

    What is the correlation coefficient?   **r** = _____

    Is this a positive or a negative correlation? (circle one)   Positive   Negative

    Based on these results, how would you explain the relationship between married couples and education?

2. Create the following scatterplot:

    Dependent variable: **74** or **%CLINTON92**

    Independent variable: **28** or **COUPLES**

    Write down the long label for **74** or **%CLINTON92** (*press* **Y** to see it):

    _____

    _____

    What is the correlation coefficient?   **r** = _____

    Is this a positive or a negative correlation? (circle one)   Positive   Negative

    Might this be a cause-and-effect relationship? Suggest why or why not.

3. Create the following scatterplot:

    Dependent variable: **43** or **ADOPTION**

    Independent variable: **25** or **%SINGLE**

    Write down the long label for **43** or **ADOPTION** (*press* **Y** to see it):

    _____

    _____

    What is the correlation coefficient?   **r** = _____

    Is this a positive or a negative correlation? (circle one)   Positive   Negative

    How would you explain this relationship?

4. Create the following scatterplot:

      Dependent variable: **88** or **BOOK $ PER**

      Independent variable: **25** or **%SINGLE**

      Write down the long label for **88** or **BOOK $ PER** (*press* **Y** to see it):

      _____

      _____

      What is the correlation coefficient?   **r** = _____

      Is this a positive or a negative correlation? (circle one)   Positive   Negative

      Are these results what you expected? Explain.

5. Create the following scatterplot:

      Dependent variable: **85** or **PET$PER**

      Independent variable: **25** or **%SINGLE**

      Write down the long label for **85** or **PET$PER** (*press* **Y** to see it):

      _____

      _____

      What is the correlation coefficient?   **r** = _____

      Is this a positive or a negative correlation? (circle one)   Positive   Negative

      Might this be a cause-and-effect relationship? Suggest why or why not.

6. *Press <ENTER>* several times to return to the red menu. Move the highlight to **G. Correlation** and *press <ENTER>*. Use the variables **36** or **%FEM.HEAD**, **35** or **%MALE.HEAD**, **45** or **MED.FAM $**, and **46** or **%POOR.FAM** to complete the following table:

	36) %FEM.HEAD	35) %MALE.HEAD	45) MED.FAM $	46) %POOR.FAM
36) %FEM.HEAD				
35) %MALE.HEAD				
45) MED.FAM $				
46) %POOR.FAM				

Summarize the economic difference between states having high rates of male-headed homes and those with high rates of female-headed homes.

7. *Press <ENTER>* twice. Place the highlight on **F. Scatterplots** and *press <ENTER>*. This time, you can select your own dependent variable. What is one variable that you think will be positively or negatively related to the percentage of the population that is married? (**Reminder:** You can use **F3** to see a list of the variables, or you can consult the list of variables in the back of your book and type in the name or number of the variable you wish to select.)

Dependent variable: _____

Independent variable: **28** or **COUPLES**

Write down the long label for your dependent variable (*press* **Y** to see it):

_____

_____

What is the correlation coefficient?   **r** = _____

Is this a positive or a negative correlation? (circle one)   Positive   Negative

Press **P** (for Print). (**Note:** If your computer is not connected to a printer or if you have been instructed not to use the printer, skip these printing instructions). Attach a copy of your results.

Describe the results of your analysis. Were these the results you expected? Explain.

✦ CHAPTER 3 ✦

Family Values

We have examined variations in family structure and the ways they correlate with other social phenomena. Now we will explore what people think about the family.

During the 1980s, and continuing into the '90s, the concept of family values has become a part of our political dialogue. Discussions concerning abortion, violence on television, tax reform, sex education, and a host of other topics have all been linked with the concern for family values. But what exactly are family values? Are they a list of political policy positions, or is the concept broader than that? For the purposes of this chapter, we will bypass the political debate and will take the concept of family values quite literally. We will define *family values* as the importance people place on being married and having children. By defining family values in this manner, we will be able to compare the importance people place on the family with the importance they place on other aspects of their lives. Then we can look at how the variations in the importance people place on the family are related to variations in lifestyles and attitudes.

Start Student MicroCase as described in the *Introduction* section at the beginning of the book. At the **DATA AND FILE MANAGEMENT MENU**, place the highlight on **I. Open, List, Erase or Copy File** and *press <ENTER>*. Now place the highlight on **NORC** (an acronym for the *National Opinion Research Center*) and *press <ENTER>* to open this file.

The screen tells you that you have opened data selected from the 1993 and 1994 General Social Surveys, which consist of a national sample of 4,598 Americans aged 18 and over, each of whom was interviewed at length.

Press <ENTER> to continue, go to the **STATISTICAL ANALYSIS MENU** (the red menu), place the highlight on the **Univariate Statistics** function, and *press <ENTER>*. Use **82** or **IMP:MARRY** as the variable. When you are asked for a subset variable, simply *press <ENTER>* to continue. This pie chart will appear:

HOW IMPORTANT TO YOU: Being married?

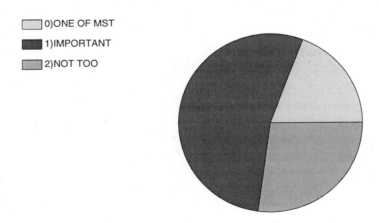

- 0)ONE OF MST
- 1)IMPORTANT
- 2)NOT TOO

Press **D** (for Distribution). This distribution will appear:

	FREQUENCY	%
ONE OF MST[1]	305	19.2
IMPORTANT	851	53.6
NOT TOO	431	27.2

Here we see that 305 persons, or 19.2 percent of the sample, said that being married is one of the most important aspects of life. An additional 53.6 percent ranked being married as being important, although other areas of their lives were more highly valued. A fairly sizable 27.2 percent responded that being married is not an important part of life. *Press <ENTER>* twice to return to the initial prompt.

Now let's see how having children is rated. Select **83** or **IMP:KIDS** as the variable. *Press <ENTER>* to skip the subset option. After the pie chart appears, *type* **D**.

	FREQUENCY	%
MOST IMPOR	375	23.7
IMPORTANT	915	57.8
LESS IMPOR	294	18.6

This distribution is very similar to that of the previous variable. We see that 23.7 percent of the sample rated having children as one of the most important parts of their lives and 57.8 percent indicated that it was important to them. Only 18.6 percent said having children was not too important to them. *Press <ENTER>* twice to return to the prompt.

The results we have looked at thus far demonstrate that Americans place a great deal of value on being married and having children. This is not surprising, since we have seen in the previous exercises that most of the population is married. A more interesting finding might come from comparing the importance Americans place on the family with the importance they place on other aspects of their lives—such as financial security, independence, and religion.

Let's look first at the importance of financial security. Select variable **84** or **IMP:FINAN**. After the pie chart appears, *type* **D**. This table appears on your screen:

	FREQUENCY	%
MOST IMPOR	427	26.9
IMPORTANT	1107	69.7
LESS IMPORT	55	3.5

In this sample, 26.9 percent rated financial security as one of the most important aspects of their lives. An additional 69.7 percent rated it at the next level of importance. Notice that these percentages are higher than the family-related value scores. *Press <ENTER>* twice to return to the prompt.

---

[1] Since MicroCase limits variable names and categories to 10 characters, some variable information is purposely shortened or misspelled. To be consistent with the software, the same spelling is generally used in the text whenever variable names and categories are referred to. (In this case, the word "most" has been shortened to "mst.")

Americans are known for the value they place on self-sufficiency and on not being dependent on others. To see the importance of this value, examine the distribution for variable **85** or **IMP:NOT DP**. Here is what you will find:

	FREQUENCY	%
MOST IMPOR	705	44.4
IMPORTANT	857	54.0
LESS IMPOR	26	1.6

As we would expect, this is a very important value in American society—44.4 percent said that being self-sufficient was one of the most important values in life. That is almost twice the number who placed the same value on being married or having children.

Finally, select variable **86** or **IMP:GOD** to see the importance of a person's religious faith. You will find these results:

	FREQUENCY	%
MOST IMPOR	733	46.2
IMPORTANT	695	43.8
LESS IMPOR	158	10.0

Faith in God was ranked by more people as one of the most important things in their lives (46.2 percent) than any of the other variables we have seen.

Although the respondents in this sample valued being married and having children, most of them valued financial security, a fulfilling job, independence, or religious faith even more.

The survey items we have examined thus far have focused on individual attitudes of respondents. Most social researchers like to go beyond describing individual attitudes by looking for the connections between ideas and actions. For example, one could hypothesize that **those who are single will be more likely to say that being married is not too important to them**. We can use data from these same data files to test this simple hypothesis.

Return to the **STATISTICAL ANALYSIS MENU**, place the highlight on **Tabular Analysis**, and *press <ENTER>*. When you are asked for the name or number of the row variable, *type* **82** or **IMP:MARRY**. This time, when you are asked for the name or number of the column variable, *type* **5** or **SINGLE/MAR**. When you are asked for a control variable, simply *press <ENTER>*. When you are asked for a subset variable, *press <ENTER>* again.

These results appear on your screen:

	NEVER MARR	MARRIED
ONE OF MST	27	278
IMPORTANT	153	698
NOT TOO	119	311

Across the top is the variable separating those who have never married from those who are, or have been, married. Down the side are the labels representing the importance of being married.

The numbers within the table reflect the numbers of single or married persons who gave each answer on the importance-of-marriage question.

Looking at the first column in the table we see that of the 299 persons who have never married, 27 said being married is one of the most important aspects of their lives, 153 said being married is important, and 119 said being married was not too important. As we would expect, not too many people who have never married rank being married as one of their most important values. But it is also interesting to note that being married is not their least important value either. Now compare the difference between those who have never married and those who have married. Of those who have been married at some time, 278 said being married is one of the most important aspects of their lives, 698 said being married is important, and 311 said being married is not too important. You will undoubtedly notice that there are more married people than never-married people who say being married is important to them. The trouble with this comparison is that there are far more married respondents (1,287 total respondents) than there are respondents who have never married (299 total respondents).

This makes it obvious that we can't simply compare raw numbers. We must take differences in the size of the populations into account. To do so, we can calculate the **percentage** of single and married persons in each category. To do that, simply *press* **C** (for Column percentages). The screen shows these results:

	NEVER MARR	MARRIED
ONE OF MST	9.0	21.6
IMPORTANT	51.2	54.2
NOT TOO	39.8	24.2

Now we more easily see the connection between having never been married and the value one places on marriage. Across the top row we see that among those who have never married, only 9 percent say that being married is one of the most important aspects of their lives, as compared to 21.6 percent of those who have married. Looking across the bottom row we see that 39.8 percent of those who have never married say being married is not too important, as compared to 24.2 percent among those who have married. Of course, we do not know which came first, the action or the attitude. It could be that those people who place a high value on marriage are more likely to seek out a marriage partner actively, whereas those who place less value on marriage engage in other pursuits. In this case, that attitude would be shaping the action. On the other hand, those who marry learn to place a high value on marriage through interaction with their spouse and others. If this is true, it is the action that determines the attitude. There are social scientists who adhere to each of these perspectives. The data available for these exercises do not allow us to determine time sequences, so you will have to choose the approach you think is most plausible.

We have seen that there is a relationship between having never married and the value one places on marriage. Now let's see whether the same holds true for divorce. Does going through a divorce influence the value one places on being married? Let's test the hypothesis that **those who have been divorced are more likely than those who have never been divorced to say that being married is not too important.**

Press <ENTER> to run a new table. This time, let's use the **F3** window to select the variables. *Press* **F3**. Use the **page down** and **down arrow** keys to place the highlight on variable **82** or **IMP:MARRY**. *Press* the **left arrow** key to select it as the row variable. Now place the highlight on **7** or **EVER DIVOR** and *press* the **left arrow** key to select it as the column variable. *Press*

<ENTER>. The two indicated variables will take their places on the screen as the row and column variables. *Press <ENTER>* again, and then again, and the table will appear. *Press* **C** (for Column percentages).

	YES	NO
ONE OF MST	24.9	27.7
IMPORTANT	59.2	59.1
NOT TOO	16.0	13.3

Here we see (by reading across and comparing) that those who have been divorced (24.9 percent) are slightly less likely than those who have never been divorced (27.7 percent) to say that being married is one of the most important aspects of their lives. Those who have been divorced (16 percent) also are slightly more likely than those who have not been divorced (13.3 percent) to say that being married is not too important. Although there appears to be a pattern, suggesting that going through a divorce decreases the importance placed on marriage, most of the differences are rather small. Small differences raise questions for survey data analysis.

Random sampling is the basis of all survey research. Rather than interview all the members of a population, survey researchers interview only a sample. As long as this sample is selected randomly, so that all members have an equal chance of being selected, the results based on the sample can be generalized to the entire population. That is, the laws of probability allow us to **calculate the odds** that something observed in the sample accurately reflects a feature of the population sampled—subject to two limitations.

First of all, the sample must be **sufficiently large**. Obviously, we couldn't use a sample of two people as the basis for describing the American population: there is a very high probability that they both would be married. For this reason, survey studies include enough cases so that they can accurately reflect the population in terms of variations in such characteristics as age, sex, education, race, religion, and so on. The accuracy of a sample is a function of its size: the larger the sample, the more accurate it is. Good survey studies are based on 1,000 cases or more. This sample is based on 4,598 Americans.

The second limitation has to do with the **magnitude of the difference** observed in a table. Because samples are based on the principle of random selection, they are subject to some degree of fluctuation. That is, for purely random reasons, there can be small differences between the sample and the population. Thus, whenever we examine cross-tabulations such as those shown above, social scientists must always ask whether they are seeing a real difference, one that would turn up if the entire population were examined, or only a random fluctuation, which does not reflect a true difference in the population.

The small size of the differences between the value placed on marriage by those who have been divorced and those who have not been divorced would make any experienced analyst suspect that the differences observed are merely the result of random fluctuations.

Fortunately, there is a very simple technique for calculating the odds that a given difference is real or random. This calculation is called a **test of statistical significance**. You will (hopefully) recall that we dealt with statistical significance back in Exercise 2 when working with data based on the 50 states. The test of statistical significance for survey data works on the same principle. Differences observed in survey samples are said to be statistically significant when the odds against the results being random are high enough. But through the years, social scientists have settled on the rule of thumb that they will ignore all differences unless the odds are at least **20 to 1** against their being random. To put it another way, social scientists reject all findings when the probability that they are random is greater than .05 (5 in 100). This level of significance means that if 100 random samples were drawn independently from the same population, a difference that large would not turn up more than five times, purely by chance. In fact, many social scientists think this too lenient a standard and some even require that the probability that a finding is random be less than .01 (1 in 100). To apply these rules of thumb, social scientists calculate the **levels of significance** of the differences in question and compare them against these standards.

Let's see what the level of significance is for this table. *Press* **S** (for Statistics). Across the screen, under the words **Nominal Statistics**, we see: **Chi-Square: 1.363 DF: 2 (Prob. = 0.506)**. Chi-Square is the name of the particular test of significance we are using. You can ignore everything else except (Prob. = 0.506), which indicates the probability that this is a random result. Put another way, this means that if there is no difference in the value placed on marriage among those who have been divorced and those who have not been divorced, we would expect an observed difference this large by sheer chance 506 times out of every 1,000 random samples, or about 50 times out of every 100 samples. This level of significance falls very short of the minimal .05 standard. So the odds are quite high that being divorced does not affect the importance one places on marriage. Because the probability is *larger* than .05, we must reject our hypothesis that **those who have been divorced are more likely than those who have never been divorced to say that being married is not too important**. The mere fact that someone has divorced at some point does not imply that the person places less importance on marriage.

Let's do another comparison. This time we will use what we have learned about probability to see whether Republicans and Democrats differ with regard to the importance they place on being married. Because the phrase *family values* has been used more in the discourse of the Republican party, our hypothesis will be that **Republicans are more likely than Democrats to say that being married is one of their most important values**. *Press <ENTER>* twice to clear the results for this analysis. Use **82** or **IMP:MARRY** as the row variable and **77** or **REP/DEM** as the column variable. *Press <ENTER>* until the table appears and then *press* **C** (for Column percentages).

	DEMOCRAT	REPUBLICAN
ONE OF MST	18.8	22.0
IMPORTANT	53.6	54.7
NOT TOO	27.6	23.4

In order to say that a hypothesis is supported, we must be able to answer two questions affirmatively. The first question is: Are the results consistent with the hypothesis? To answer that question, we need to look at the column percentages in the table. Notice that 18.8 percent of Democrats say that being married is one of their most important values. Moving across the table, we see that 22 percent of Republicans hold this view. In this case, the difference between Republicans and Democrats is so small that we would have to question the support these findings provide for our hypothesis.

The second question we must be able to answer affirmatively is: Are the results statistically significant? *Press* **S** (for Statistics). Here we see Prob. = 0.134, which is greater than the allowed probability of .05. Therefore, we must answer *no* to the second question; the differences in the percentages are not large enough to be statistically significant. Even though the direction of the findings was somewhat consistent with the hypothesis, our hypothesis must be rejected. Republicans and Democrats may disagree on what social policies need to be enacted to most benefit families, but there is not a statistically significant difference in the value they place on the family itself. Some people who believe being married is one of the most important aspects of their lives are Republicans; others are Democrats.

So far, we have seen that although many people consider being married and having children to be the most important value in their lives, even more place a higher priority on other values. The relationship between the value one places on being married and other family values and attitudes is somewhat varied. Although having never been married is related to the value one places on marriage, having ever divorced is not. Nor is the value one places on the family related to being a Republican or a Democrat. Thus, we can conclude that there is diversity with regard to the importance of family values, but there is also diversity among those who hold similar family values. In the exercises that follow, you will have a chance to explore the ways family values are related to some other social and demographic characteristics.

Your turn.

WORKSHEET

NAME:

COURSE:

DATE:

EXERCISE
3

If you have not done so already, start MicroCase and open the **NORC** data file.

1. If the importance of marriage in our society is declining, then: **Young people will place less importance on being married than those who are older.**

    Select **B. Tabular Statistics**. Make variable **82** or **IMP:MARRY** the row variable and **2** or **AGE** the column variable. *Press <ENTER>* twice and *type* **C** (for Column percentages). Fill in the percentaged results below. (**Note:** Use the **right arrow** key to view the last column.)

	18–29	30–39	40–49	50–64	65 & OVER
ONE OF MST	%	%	%	%	%
IMPORTANT	%	%	%	%	%
NOT TOO	%	%	%	%	%

    Is the difference statistically significant? (circle one) Yes No

    Is the hypothesis supported or rejected? (circle one) Supported Rejected

    Based on these results, do you believe the value our society places on the family is declining? Explain.

2. The hypothesis is: **Women will place more importance on marriage than will men.**

    Make variable **82** or **IMP:MARRY** the row variable and **1** or **SEX** the column variable. *Press <ENTER>* twice and *type* **C** (for Column percentages). Fill in the table below.

	MALE	FEMALE
ONE OF MST	%	%
IMPORTANT	%	%
NOT TOO	%	%

Is the difference statistically significant? (circle one)   Yes   No

Is the hypothesis supported or rejected? (circle one)   Supported   Rejected

The hypothesis is: **Women will place more importance on having children than will men.**

Make variable **83** or **IMP:KIDS** the row variable and **1** or **SEX** the column variable. At the final table *type* **C** (for Column percentages). Fill in the table below.

	MALE	FEMALE
MOST IMPOR	%	%
IMPORTANT	%	%
LESS IMPOR	%	%

Is the difference statistically significant? (circle one)   Yes   No

Is the hypothesis supported or rejected? (circle one)   Supported   Rejected

Do the results of the last two tables surprise you? Explain.

3. Create and fill in the table below. Make variable **82** or **IMP:MARRY** the row variable and **30** or **CLASS** the column variable. At the final table *type* **C** (for Column percentages). Fill in the table below.

	LOWER	WORKING	MIDDLE	UPPER
ONE OF MST	%	%	%	%
IMPORTANT	%	%	%	%
LESS IMPOR	%	%	%	%

Is the difference statistically significant? (circle one)   Yes   No

Can you suggest a reason for this particular outcome?

4. The hypothesis is: **Those who attend church weekly will place more importance on being married.**

    Make variable **82** or **IMP:MARRY** the row variable and **49** or **CH.ATTEND** the column variable. At the final table *type* **C** (for Column percentages). Fill in the table below.

	LESS OFTEN	ANNUALLY	MONTHLY	WEEKLY
ONE OF MST	%	%	%	%
IMPORTANT	%	%	%	%
NOT TOO	%	%	%	%

Is the difference statistically significant? (circle one) Yes No

Is the hypothesis supported or rejected? (circle one) Supported Rejected

The hypothesis is: **Religious fundamentalists will place more importance on being married than will liberal denominations.**

Use the **F3** key to look at the complete description for **52) R.FUND/LIB**. Make variable **82** or **IMP:MARRY** the row variable and **52** or **R.FUND/LIB** the column variable. At the final table *type* **C** (for Column percentages). Fill in the table below.

	FUNDAMENT.	MODERATE	LIBERAL
ONE OF MST	%	%	%
IMPORTANT	%	%	%
NOT TOO	%	%	%

Is the difference statistically significant? (circle one) Yes No

Is the hypothesis supported or rejected? (circle one)   Supported   Rejected

How would you summarize the relationship between religion and the perceived importance of marriage?

5. The hypothesis is: **Those who place the most value on being married will be the most likely to believe that premarital sex is always wrong.**

Make variable **66** or **PREM.SEX** the row variable and **82** or **IMP:MARRY** the column variable. At the final table *type* **C** (for Column percentages). Fill in the table below.

	ONE OF MST	IMPORTANT	NOT TOO
ALWAYS	%	%	%
ALMOST AL.	%	%	%
SOMETIMES	%	%	%
NOT WRONG	%	%	%

Is the difference statistically significant? (circle one)   Yes   No

Is the hypothesis supported or rejected? (circle one)   Supported   Rejected

How would you explain these results?

6. Use **F3** to look at the complete description for **76) EDUCATE $**. The hypothesis is: **Those who place the most importance on having children will be more likely to believe the government spends too little on education.**

Make variable **76** or **EDUCATE $** the row variable and **83** or **IMP:KIDS** the column variable. At the final table *type* **C** (for Column percentages). Fill in the table below.

	MOST IMPOR	IMPORTANT	LESS IMPOR
TOO LITTLE	%	%	%
RIGHT	%	%	%
TOO MUCH	%	%	%

Is the difference statistically significant? (circle one) Yes No

Is the hypothesis supported or rejected? (circle one) Supported Rejected

Were these the results you expected? Explain.

7. Now it's time to test your own hypothesis using the importance of having children as the independent variable and a variable of your choice as the dependent variable. Remember, you can use **F3** to view and select variables, or you can consult the list of variables in the back of your book and type in the name or number of the variable you wish to select.

   Select a variable that you believe will be dependent on, or affected by, the importance people place on having children. Make this your row variable.

   Which variable did you select? _____

Make **83** or **IMP:KIDS** the column variable.

   What is your hypothesis? (You can consider the hypotheses used in this exercise as examples.)

   _____

   _____

   Type **C** (for Column percentages). *Press* **P** (for Print). (**Note:** If your computer is not connected to a printer, or you have been instructed not to use the printer, skip these printing instructions. Instead, draw a table on a separate sheet of paper showing the final percentaged results you obtained.) Attach a copy of the results.

Is the difference statistically significant? (circle one)   Yes   No

Is the hypothesis supported or rejected? (circle one)   Supported   Rejected

Discuss why you think your hypothesis was, or was not, supported.

◆ CHAPTER 4 ◆
Premarital Sex

Sociologist Ira Reiss has described four moral standards of premarital sexuality. The first is the *abstinence standard,* which is the belief that premarital sexual intercourse is wrong for both men and women, regardless of their feelings for each other. This was the most commonly held sexual standard in the U.S. until the 1950s or 1960s. The second is what Reiss calls the *double standard,* or the belief that premarital intercourse is permissible for men but not for women. Although not widely discussed publicly, this has been a very common standard until perhaps just recently. The third is *permissiveness with affection,* which is the belief that premarital intercourse is acceptable as long as the couple has an affectionate, stable relationship. *Permissiveness with or without affection* is the fourth standard. As the name suggests, this is the belief that premarital sex is never wrong as long as it is consensual. Which of these beliefs do you hold? The available data do not allow us to clearly examine each of these four standards, but we can use some other questions to arrive at some understanding of what Americans believe about premarital sexual intercourse. Along the way, we will look for variations in the beliefs held by different groups.

Start MicroCase and open the **NORC** data file. Place the highlight on **A. Univariate Statistics** and *press <ENTER>*. When you are asked for the name or number of the variable you wish to examine, *type* **66** or **PREM.SEX** and *press <ENTER>* twice. The following pie chart will appear on your screen:

If a man and a woman have sex relations before marriage, do you think it is always wrong, almost always wrong, wrong only sometimes, or not wrong at all?

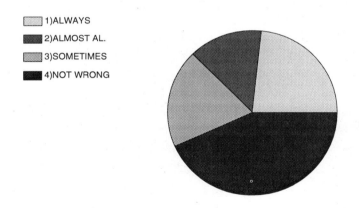

1)ALWAYS
2)ALMOST AL.
3)SOMETIMES
4)NOT WRONG

Type **T** (for Table) to look at the distribution.

	FREQUENCY	%
ALWAYS	823	23.5
ALMOST AL.	491	14.0
SOMETIMES	670	19.1
NOT WRONG	1524	43.4

The responses are fairly divided, but the largest group consists of those who believe premarital sex is not wrong (43.4 percent). This group would probably express a view similar to Reiss' *permissiveness with or without affection* moral standard. On the other hand, the second largest group consists of those who believe premarital sex is always wrong (23.5 percent). These respondents would be in the *abstinence* category. Among the rest of the respondents, 19.1 percent believe premarital sex is sometimes wrong and 14 percent believe it is almost always wrong. These respondents are probably closest to Reiss' *permissiveness with affection* standard.

Press <ENTER> several times to return to the statistics menu, then select **B. Tabular Statistics**. Tabular statistics will allow us to see which variables help explain the variation in attitudes toward premarital sex. For example, because single persons are affected most by this issue, let's test the hypothesis that **people who have never been married will be less likely to believe that premarital sex is always wrong.** The independent variable in this hypothesis is marital status; the dependent variable is attitude toward premarital sex. Therefore, when you are asked for the name or number of the row variable, *type* **66** or **PREM.SEX** and *press <ENTER>*. When asked for the name or number of the column variable, *type* **5** or **SINGLE/MAR** and *press <ENTER>* several times until the table appears. *Press* **C** (for Column percentages).

	NEVER MARR	MARRIED
ALWAYS	14.2	25.9
ALMOST AL.	13.2	14.2
SOMETIMES	23.1	18.1
NOT WRONG	49.6	41.9

As we saw in the previous exercise, to gain support for a hypothesis we must be able to answer two questions affirmatively. The first question is: Are the results consistent with the hypothesis? To answer that question, we need to look at the column percentages in the table. As we read across the top row in this table, we see that 14.2 percent of those who are single believe premarital sex is always wrong, while 25.9 percent who have married hold this belief. Hence, the results are consistent with the stated hypothesis.

The second question we must be able to answer affirmatively is: Are the results statistically significant? *Press* **S** (for Statistics). Here we see that Prob. = 0.000. This shows that the odds of getting differences this large between the groups being compared (in this case, those who are married and those who are not married) is less than 1 in 1,000. Since this probability is below the .05 level, we can say that our hypothesis is supported.

It is commonly believed that men are more willing than women to engage in premarital sex. Does this mean that fewer men believe premarital sex is wrong? *Press <ENTER>* twice to get ready to run a new table. When you are asked for the name or number of the row variable, *type* **66** or **PREM.SEX** and *press <ENTER>*. When prompted for the name or number of the column variable, *type* **1** or **SEX** and *press <ENTER>* several times until the table appears. *Press* **C** (for Column percentages). The hypothesis is: **Men are less likely than women to believe that premarital sex is always wrong.**

	MALE	FEMALE
ALWAYS	20.0	26.1
ALMOST AL.	13.3	14.5
SOMETIMES	18.2	19.8
NOT WRONG	48.5	39.5

The direction of the findings is consistent with the hypothesis: 20 percent of the men believe pre-marital sex is always wrong, by comparison with 26.1 percent of the women who hold this belief. In fact, almost half the men (48.5 percent) believe premarital sex is never wrong. *Press* **S** (for Statistics). The Prob. = 0.000, which means the difference is statistically significant and the hypothesis is supported. Men are less disapproving of premarital sex than are women.

The three institutions that play the most direct role in shaping our personal values are the family, the church, and the school. The extent to which any of these institutions deliberately teach sexual values, and the values they do teach, vary greatly. Not all parents will discuss sexual issues with their children, and the values that are taught will not all be the same. The same is true for churches and schools: both the amount of teaching that takes place and the material that is taught will vary from one church or school to the next. But can some of the variation in attitudes toward premarital sex be explained by taking into account the influence of these three social institutions?

Earlier it was demonstrated that a respondent's current marital status influences his or her attitude toward premarital sex—but what about the structure of the family that person was socialized into? Is being raised in a two-parent home, as opposed to a one-parent home, a predictor of sexual attitudes? *Press <ENTER>* twice to clear the screen for a new table. Use **66** or **PREM.SEX** as the row variable. Variable **25) FAM @ 16** asked respondents if, at the age of 16, they lived with both of their parents. Select this variable as the column variable. When the final table appears, *press* **C** (for Column percentages).

	NO	YES
ALWAYS	21.6	24.2
ALMOST AL.	13.3	14.3
SOMETIMES	18.9	19.2
NOT WRONG	46.2	42.3

The percentages are very close, but a pattern can be seen. Among those who were not living with both parents at age 16, 21.6 percent believe premarital sex is always wrong, by comparison with 24.2 percent for those who were living with both parents at age 16. We see about the same difference at the other end of the spectrum. Forty-six percent of those who were not living with both parents believe premarital sex is not wrong, compared to 42.3 percent of those who were living with both parents. *Press* **S** (for Statistics). The difference is not statistically significant (Prob. = 0.161).

The second agent of socialization to explore is the church. Select **66** or **PREM.SEX** as the row variable and **49** or **CH.ATTEND** as the column variable. (Make sure to always percentage the final table properly.) The hypothesis is: **People who attend church on a regular basis will be more likely to believe that premarital sex is always wrong.** Here are the results:

	LESS OFTEN	ANNUALLY	MONTHLY	WEEKLY
ALWAYS	15.0	13.7	18.2	40.7
ALMOST AL.	9.6	12.0	16.3	17.4
SOMETIMES	18.1	21.4	20.7	17.4
NOT WRONG	57.4	52.9	44.9	24.4

The largest difference is between those who attend church weekly and the rest of the categories. Forty percent of the weekly attendees believe premarital sex is always wrong. This is more than twice the percentage for those who attend monthly (18.2 percent), annually (13.7 percent), or less than once per year (15 percent). *Type* **S** (for Statistics). The Prob. = 0.000. The hypothesis is supported.

The third institution that often contributes directly to sexual socialization is the school. Because educational institutions tend to encourage students to challenge traditional ideas and norms, **the more educated a person is, the less likely he or she is to believe that premarital sex is always wrong.** Use **66** or **PREM.SEX** as the row variable and **42** or **DEGREE** as the column variable. The percentaged results look like this:

	NOT H.S.	HIGH SCH.	JR. COL.	B.A.	GRAD. DEG.
ALWAYS	33.8	23.9	19.8	18.3	13.3
ALMOST AL.	13.1	14.7	9.4	14.6	12.5
SOMETIMES	16.9	18.0	20.8	23.6	20.5
NOT WRONG	36.2	43.5	50.0	43.5	53.8

As the level of education rises, the percentage who disapprove of premarital sex declines. For example, 33.8 percent of those who did not finish high school believe premarital sex is always wrong, as compared with only 18.3 percent for those who hold bachelor degrees. (Use the **right arrow** key to see the results for those with graduate degrees.) *Press* **S** (for Statistics). The Prob. = 0.000, so the difference is statistically significant. The hypothesis is supported—higher education is associated with more permissive sexual attitudes.

In examining the variations in attitudes toward premarital sex, we have found that current marital status, gender, church attendance, and education are all significant predictors of premarital sexual attitudes in varying degrees. The dependent variable in each of the preceding tables was one's attitude toward premarital sex in general. But how do people feel about young teens having premarital sex? Return to the main menu and move the highlight to **A. Univariate Statistics**. When you are asked for the name or number of a variable, *type* **65** or **TEEN SEX?** and *press <ENTER>* twice. This pie chart will appear:

If a male and a female in their early teens, say 14 to 16 years old, have sex relations before marriage do you think it is always wrong, almost always wrong, wrong only sometimes, or not wrong at all?

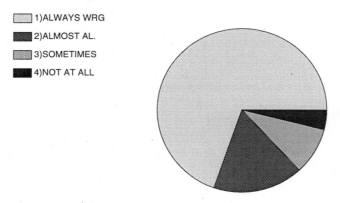

1)ALWAYS WRG
2)ALMOST AL.
3)SOMETIMES
4)NOT AT ALL

Type **T** (for Table). This will be your distribution:

	FREQUENCY	%
ALWAYS WRG	2096	69.6
ALMOST AL.	522	17.3
SOMETIMES	278	9.2
NOT AT ALL	116	3.9

By comparison with the prior results that showed that 25 percent of adult Americans who believe that premarital sex for people of all ages is always wrong, 69 percent of those surveyed believe that premarital sex is always wrong for those in their early teens. Less than 4 percent of the respondents believe that premarital sex for this age group is never wrong, by comparison with the 41 percent who would say that about premarital sex in general. Thus, premarital sexual standards in general are fairly permissive, but most people believe it is better for those in their young teens to wait until marriage to have sex.

Thus far, the focus has been on the attitudes of an adult population regarding issues pertaining to sexuality. Now we will turn our attention to people's actual behavior. To do so, we will be using data from the National Survey of Children. Return to the main menu and *type S* to switch to the **DATA AND FILE MANAGEMENT MENU**. Place the highlight on **I. Open, List, Erase or Copy File** and *press <ENTER>*. Move the highlight to **NSC** and *press <ENTER>*. You will see that this survey data consists of 1,249 cases and 29 variables. These data were taken from the National Survey of Children, which was conducted by Child Trends, Inc. Interviews were conducted with each child on three different occasions over an 11-year time span. The first interview took place in 1976, when the children were between the ages of 7 and 11. The second interview was in 1981. The final interview was conducted in 1987. One of each child's parents, and in some cases one of the child's teachers, was also interviewed. *Press <ENTER>* to continue.

Go to the **STATISTICAL ANALYSIS MENU** and select **A. Univariate Statistics**. When you are asked for the name or number of the variable you wish to examine, *type* **22** or **AGE.1.SEX** and *press <ENTER>* twice. A pie graph will appear on your screen. *Type* **T** (for Table). The following appears:

	FREQUENCY	%
15 & UNDER	203	18.0
16	224	19.8
17	218	19.3
18+/NOT	485	42.9

The data for this variable were taken from the final interview, when the respondents were between 18 and 22 years old. They were asked at what age they first had sexual intercourse. Looking at the results, we see that 18 percent had intercourse before or at the age of 15, 19.8 percent at age 16, and 19.3 percent at age 17. The final category (18+/NOT) includes those individuals who either waited until they were "legal adults" to have sex or had abstained from sex completely.

In the exercises that follow, you will have the opportunity to explain some of the variation in the ages at which the respondents became sexually active. We will be using information collected during the second and third interviews. The data from the second interview will reveal to us the respondents' perceptions of their family life during the time when most of them were becoming sexually active. The data from the third interview include their recollections of the time and the nature of each respondent's initial sexual encounter. Comparing these data will help us understand more about premarital sexual activity and its relationship to family life.

WORKSHEET

NAME: _____

COURSE: _____

DATE: _____

Workbook exercises and software are copyrighted. Copying is prohibited by law.

EXERCISE
4

Open the **NSC SURVEY** data file and select the **Tabular Statistics** function.

1. The hypothesis is: **Men will have become sexually active at an earlier age than women.**

   Make **22** or **AGE.1.SEX** the row variable and **4** or **GENDER** the column variable. *Press* **C** (for Column percentages). Fill in the table.

	MALE	FEMALE
15 & UNDER	%	%
16	%	%
17	%	%
18+/NOT	%	%

   Prob. = _____

   Is the difference statistically significant? (circle one)　　　　　　Yes　　No

   Is the hypothesis supported or rejected? (circle one)　　　Supported　　Rejected

2. The hypothesis is: **Those who did not attend church regularly as teens will have become sexually active at an earlier age.**

   Make **22** or **AGE.1.SEX** the row variable and **26** or **CH.ATTEND** the column variable. *Press* **C** (for Column percentages). Fill in the table.

	WEEKLY	1/MONTH	FEW/YR	NEVER
15 & UNDER	%	%	%	%
16	%	%	%	%
17	%	%	%	%
18+/NOT	%	%	%	%

   Prob. = _____

Is the difference statistically significant? (circle one)   Yes   No

Is the hypothesis supported or rejected? (circle one)   Supported   Rejected

3. Because people with more education have more permissive sexual attitudes, **people with a higher level of education will have become sexually active at an earlier age.**

Make **22** or **AGE.1.SEX** the row variable and **14** or **DEGREE** the column variable. *Press* **C** (for Column percentages). Fill in the table.

	< HIGH SCH	HIGH SCH	COLLEGE
15 & UNDER	%	%	%
16	%	%	%
17	%	%	%
18+/NOT	%	%	%

Prob. = _____

Is the difference statistically significant? (circle one)   Yes   No

Is the hypothesis supported or rejected? (circle one)   Supported   Rejected

In the introduction to this exercise, it was demonstrated that people with more education tend to have more permissive sexual attitudes. How would you explain the relationship between those findings and the results of this hypothesis?

4. Let's consider the family income of the child's parents. Make **22** or **AGE.1.SEX** the row variable and **2** or **FAMILY $** the column variable. *Press* **C** (for Column percentages). Create and fill in the table below.

	BELOW AVER	AVERAGE	ABOVE AVER
15 & UNDER	%	%	%
16	%	%	%
17	%	%	%
18+/NOT	%	%	%

Prob. = _____

Is the difference statistically significant? (circle one)   Yes   No

Summarize the results of this table in one or two sentences. Then explain why you think these results occur.

5. The hypothesis is: **Those who were raised in two-parent families will be less likely to have become sexually active at a younger age.**

Make **22** or **AGE.1.SEX** the row variable and **1** or **TWO-PARENT** the column variable. *Press* **C** (for Column percentages). Fill in the table.

	TWO-PARENT	ONE-PARENT
15 & UNDER	%	%
16	%	%
17	%	%
18+/NOT	%	%

Prob. = _____

Is the difference statistically significant? (circle one) Yes No

Is the hypothesis supported or rejected? (circle one) Supported Rejected

6. The hypothesis is: **Those who say they had rules about dating when they were teenagers will be less likely to have become sexually active at an earlier age.**

Make **22** or **AGE.1.SEX** the row variable and **20** or **DATE.RULES** the column variable. *Press* **C** (for Column percentages). Fill in the table.

	YES	NO
15 & UNDER	%	%
16	%	%
17	%	%
18+/NOT	%	%

Prob. = _____

Is the difference statistically significant? (circle one) Yes No

Is the hypothesis supported or rejected? (circle one) Supported Rejected

7. The hypothesis is: **Those who said they had close relationships with their mothers as teenagers will be less likely to have become sexually active at an earlier age.**

Make **22** or **AGE.1.SEX** the row variable and **11** or **CLOSE.MOM** the column variable. *Press* **C** (for Column percentages). Fill in the table.

	EXTREMELY	QUITE	FAIRLY	NOT VERY
15 & UNDER	%	%	%	%
16	%	%	%	%
17	%	%	%	%
18+/NOT	%	%	%	%

Prob. = _____

Is the difference statistically significant? (circle one) Yes No

Is the hypothesis supported or rejected? (circle one) Supported Rejected

8. The hypothesis is: **Those who said they had close relationships with their fathers as teenagers will be less likely to have become sexually active at an earlier age.**

   Make **22** or **AGE.1.SEX** the row variable and **12** or **CLOSE.DAD** the column variable. *Press* **C** (for Column percentages). Fill in the table.

	EXTREMELY	QUITE	FAIRLY	NOT VERY
15 & UNDER	%	%	%	%
16	%	%	%	%
17	%	%	%	%
18+/NOT	%	%	%	%

Prob. = _____

Is the difference statistically significant? (circle one)   Yes   No

Is the hypothesis supported or rejected? (circle one)   Supported   Rejected

Based on the above hypotheses (questions 5–8), what would you conclude about the relationship between parenting and premarital sexual activity?

9. Use the **F3** key to examine the complete description for **16) UNHAPPY**. Now create and fill in the table below. Make **22** or **AGE.1.SEX** the row variable and **16** or **UNHAPPY** the column variable. *Press* **C** *(for Column percentages).*

	HARDLY EVR	OCCASIONAL	OFTEN
15 & UNDER	%	%	%
16	%	%	%
17	%	%	%
18+/NOT	%	%	%

Prob. = _____

Is the difference statistically significant? (circle one)   Yes   No

Summarize the results of this table in one or two sentences. Then explain why you think these results occur.

10. Now it's time to test your own hypothesis. Remember, you can use **F3** to view and select variables, or you can consult the list of variables in the back of your book and type in the name or number of the variable you wish to select.

Write a hypothesis using **22** or **AGE.1.SEX** as either the independent (cause) or dependent (effect) variable:

_____

_____

What is your dependent variable?   _____
(make this your row variable)

What is your independent variable?   _____
(make this your column variable)

Type **C** (for Column percentages). *Press* **P** (for Print). (**Note:** If your computer is not connected to a printer, or you have been instructed not to use the printer, skip these printing instructions. Instead, draw a table on a separate sheet of paper showing the final, percentaged results you obtained.) Attach a copy of the results.

Is the difference statistically significant? (circle one)   Yes   No

Is the hypothesis supported or rejected? (circle one)   Supported   Rejected

Discuss why you think your hypothesis was, or was not, supported.

◆ CHAPTER 5 ◆

Mate Selection:
Homogamy or Heterogamy

Common wisdom offers us conflicting views on marital attraction. We are told there are lots of fish in the sea; at the same time, we are encouraged to find our *one* true love. We are told that "opposites attract" but also that "birds of a feather flock together." So what should we believe? Do we select our marriage partners from a wide pool of eligibles—or is the selection rather limited? Do opposites attract—or are people more attracted by similarities? This exercise will address these questions by comparing the social and demographic characteristics of marriage partners with each other. Social scientists refer to marriage between two people with similar social characteristics as **homogamy**; marriage between two people with dissimilar backgrounds is called **heterogamy**. By the end of this exercise, you should be able to demonstrate which of these two concepts best characterizes mate selection and marriage in our society.

Let's begin by using a measure of homogamy from the National Survey of Children. Start Student MicroCase and select **I. Open, Look, Erase or Copy File**. Move the highlight to **NSC** and *press <ENTER>*. Go to the **STATISTICAL ANALYSIS MENU** and select **A. Univariate Statistics**. When you are asked for the name or number of the variable you wish to examine, *type* **9** or **AGE-DIFF** and *press <ENTER>*. *Press <ENTER>* again to skip the subset option. This graphic will appear on your screen:

Age Difference Between Married Parents

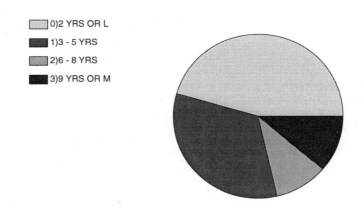

This pie chart presents the age differences between husbands and wives. The two largest groups by far are those couples who have an age difference of 2 years or less and those who have an age difference of 3 to 5 years. *Type* **D** to look at the percentage distribution. Here we see that 45 percent of all married partners are within 2 years of one another. The groups of spouses who have an age difference of 6 to 8 years, and one of more than 9 years, each account for only 10 percent of the married couples. With regard to age, most marriages are characterized by homogamy.

Press <ENTER> several times to return to the main menu. *Type* **S** to switch to the **DATA AND FILE MANAGEMENT MENU**. Open the **NORC** data file and return to the **STATISTICAL ANALYSIS MENU**. Select **B. Tabular Statistics**. If homogamy is the guiding principle behind mate selection, then a person's level of education should be an accurate predictor of his or her spouse's level of education. The hypothesis is: **People will tend to choose spouses who have the same level of education as themselves.** When you are asked for the name or number of the row variable, *type* **43** or **MATE DEGR.** and *press <ENTER>*. When you are asked for the name or number of the column variable, *type* **42** or **DEGREE** and *press <ENTER>*. *Press <ENTER>* twice to skip the control and subset variable option. *Press* **C** (for Column percentages) and this table will appear:

	NOT H.S.	HIGH SCH.	JR. COL.	B.A.	GRAD. DEG.
NOT H.S	49.0	13.2	4.7	2.5	0.5
HIGH SCH.	43.3	68.6	50.7	33.6	24.2
JR. COL.	3.6	5.2	15.3	7.1	7.0
B.A.	2.7	10.4	22.0	41.5	34.9
GRAD. DEG.	1.5	2.7	7.3	15.2	33.5

Remember, to gain support for a hypothesis we must be able to answer two questions affirmatively. The first question is: Are the results consistent with the hypothesis? To answer that question, we need to look at the column percentages in the table. Notice that 49 percent of those who have less than a high school education married someone who also had less than a high school education. Sixty-eight percent of those whose highest degree was a high school diploma married someone with a similar level of education. Forty-one percent of those with a bachelor's degree married someone similarly educated. Thirty-three percent of those with graduate degrees married people who also had earned graduate degrees. The only notable exceptions are junior college graduates. Half the junior college graduates (50.7 percent) married someone whose highest degree was a high school diploma. Because of the large number of part-time and commuter students, a junior college education may not have the same impact as a four-year college experience. But, overall, these results are quite consistent with the hypothesis.

The second question we must be able to answer affirmatively is: Are the results statistically significant? *Press* **S** (for Statistics). Here we see that Prob. = 0.000. There is less than 1 chance in 1,000 of getting differences this large by chance. So, yes, the results are statistically significant. Because the results are statistically significant and because the results are consistent with the wording of the hypothesis, we can say that our hypothesis is supported. People do tend to choose spouses with the same level of education as themselves.

Let's go back a generation and see if these findings still hold true. *Press <ENTER>* twice to clear the previous table. When you are asked for the name or number of the row variable, *type* **44** or **DAD EDUC** and *press <ENTER>*. When you are asked for the column variable, *type* **45** or **MOM EDUC** and *press <ENTER>* three times. *Press* **C** (for Column percentages). Here are the results:

	< HIGH SCH	HIGH SCH	COLLEGE
< HIGH SCH	77.6	27.6	12.4
HIGH SCH	14.8	44.7	22.1
COLLEGE	7.6	27.7	65.5

The trend appears to be consistent with the principle of homogamy. Most spouses in each category were married to people with the same level of education. In each of the columns, the highest percentage is for someone with the same level of education. Among those with less than a high school education, 77.6 percent married people who also had not completed high school. For those with a high school diploma, 44.7 percent married people with the same level of education. The percentage then goes up again for college graduates: 65.5 percent have an educationally homogamous marriage.

Type **S** (for Statistics). The probability is equal to .000, which means that the differences are statistically significant and our hypothesis is supported. There is some other useful information on this screen, which tells us more about the ways these two variables are related. In addition to showing the probability that a difference this great arose by chance, the screen shows us a correlation coefficient: V = 0.449. **V** stands for Cramer's V and is used for cross-tabulations like this to indicate the *strength* of the relationship. V is calculated much like r, the correlation coefficient invented by Pearson, which we examined in Exercise 2. It also varies from 0 (no relationship) to 1 (perfect relationship), but it cannot have a negative value like r can. For a variety of reasons that need not concern you until you take a statistics course, correlations on aggregate data tend to be much higher than those based on survey data. Thus, a V of this size is regarded as very strong.

Many factors contribute to the high incidence of educational homogamy. One would be opportunity. Many people meet their future spouses while attending school—either in high school or beyond. The influence of age homogamy would be another factor. People of a similar age are more likely to have the same level of education. Yet another factor would be childhood socialization. People who have similar levels of education probably come from homes with similar socioeconomic characteristics, where similar educational values are taught. This factor can be demonstrated by comparing the educational levels of each spouse's parents.

Press <ENTER> twice and you will be ready to run a new table.

Select **46** or **SP.DAD.ED** as the row variable and **44** or **DAD EDUC** as the column variable. When the table appears on the screen, *press* **C** (for Column percentages). The hypothesis is: **People will tend to marry someone whose parents have a level of education similar to that of their own parents.**

	< HIGH SCH	HIGH SCH	COLLEGE
< HIGH SCH	61.0	20.2	19.4
HIGH SCH	26.2	54.8	39.5
COLLEGE	12.8	25.0	41.1

The pattern is consistent with that of educational homogamy. The highest percentage is for those who married people with the same level of education: 61 percent of those with less than a high school diploma, 54.8 percent of high school graduates, and 41.1 percent of college graduates. *Press* **S** to look at the statistics. Prob. = 0.000 and V = 0.319. The hypothesis is supported: most people marry someone whose father had a level of education similar to that of their own father.

Press <ENTER> twice to get ready to run a new table.

Is the mother's level of education also a predictor of whom one is likely to marry? Try **47** or **SP.MOM.ED** as your row variable and **45** or **MOM EDUC** as your column variable. When the table appears on the screen, *press* **C** (for Column percentages) and you will see the following results:

	< HIGH SCH	HIGH SCH	COLLEGE
< HIGH SCH	47.2	20.0	9.9
HIGH SCH	31.1	58.9	67.6
COLLEGE	21.7	21.1	22.5

Overall, the trend is the same as it was for matching the fathers' levels of education. Forty-seven percent of those whose mothers did not finish high school married people whose mothers also did not finish high school. Fifty-eight percent of those whose mothers had a high school diploma married people whose mothers had the same level of education. The only exception is that 67.6 percent of the respondents whose mothers had a college education married people whose mothers had only a high school diploma. Until recently, women were far less likely than men to go to college—thereby reducing the probability that two people whose mothers had both completed college would marry.

Press **S** (for Statistics). The probability is still equal to 0.000 and Cramer's V = 0.257. Most people do marry someone whose parents had a level of education similar to that of their own parents. Because income is so closely related to education, we can conclude that most people marry someone who is from a similar socioeconomic background and one where similar educational values were expressed. It is not just current opportunities that lead to educational homogamy; it is our pattern of socialization as well.

Another indicator of the influence of socialization on mate selection comes from looking at religious upbringing. The hypothesis is: **People will tend to marry someone whose religious upbringing is similar to their own.** *Press <ENTER>* twice to get ready for a new table. This time, make **55** or **SP.FUND@16** the row variable and **54** or **R.FUND@16** the column variable. **SP.FUND@16** indicates the type of church the respondent's spouse went to at the age of 16 while **R.FUND@16** indicates the type of church that the respondent went to at the age of 16. (Those respondents or spouses who did not attend church are not included in this analysis.) When the table appears on the screen, *press* **C** (for Column percentages).

	FUNDAMENT.	MODERATE	LIBERAL
FUNDAMENT.	57.3	16.1	20.4
MODERATE	22.3	65.7	34.2
LIBERAL	20.4	18.2	41.9

It appears that most people who were raised in religious households married people with similar religious orientations. Fifty-seven percent of those who attended fundamentalist churches in their youth married people with similar religious backgrounds. Sixty-five percent of those who attended churches that would be characterized as moderate married people who attended similar churches. And 41.9 percent of those who attended more liberal churches married people with the same background. *Press* **S** (for Statistics). Prob. = 0.000, so we can conclude that these findings are not random. V = 0.341, which is indicative of a fairly strong relationship between these two variables. Our hypothesis is again supported—most people marry someone who had a similar religious upbringing.

One reason a person's religious affiliation at age 16 is so influential in mate selection is that this is when adolescents are beginning to date and many will be married in the not too distant future—but what about remarriages? Remarriages following a divorce or the death of a spouse generally occur when someone is older and has had more life experiences. Therefore, a researcher may wonder whether religious homogamy has the same impact on remarriages as it does on first marriages. This will call for the use of a **control variable**.

Press <ENTER> twice to get set for a new table. Again, make **55** or **SP.FUND@16** the row variable and **54** or **R.FUND@16** the column variable. But now, when you are asked for the name or number of control variable 1, *type* **9** or **REMARRIAGE** and *press <ENTER>* three times. When the table appears on the screen, *press* **C** (for Column percentages).

	FUNDAMENT.	MODERATE	LIBERAL
FUNDAMENT.	58.1	14.7	23.4
MODERATE	23.7	67.5	32.7
LIBERAL	18.3	17.9	43.9

At the top left of the screen, you will see **1 MARRIAGE**. This means that this table is limited to those who have been married only once. You will see that the results are very similar to those in the previous table, before the control variable was added. Most first marriages involve people with similar religious upbringings. *Press* **S** (for Statistics). The probability is statistically significant (Prob. = 0.000) and V is a relatively strong 0.361. *Press <ENTER>* once to return to the table. Now *press <ENTER>* again to see the table for those respondents who have been married more than once. *Press* **C** (for Column percentages).

	FUNDAMENT.	MODERATE	LIBERAL
FUNDAMENT.	54.4	21.4	26.2
MODERATE	18.4	59.2	38.1
LIBERAL	27.2	19.4	35.7

The results for remarriages do not appear to be that much different from those for first marriages. The only exception appears to be that religious liberals may be more likely to have heterogenous remarriages. *Press* **S** to look at the statistics. The probability still equals 0.000, but V has dipped slightly to 0.283. Remarriages are characterized by religious homogamy, although slightly less so than first marriages.

Finally, let's see if the religious homogamy hypothesis is supported for the respondent's *current* religious affiliation as well. To do this, use **53** or **SP.FUND.** as your row variable and **52** or **R.FUND/LIB** as your column variable. *Press* **C** (for Column percentages).

	FUNDAMENT.	MODERATE	LIBERAL
FUNDAMENT.	76.6	8.7	9.3
MODERATE	12.9	78.1	17.3
LIBERAL	10.5	13.2	73.4

The results are consistent with those for religious upbringing. By far the largest percentage in each column is for those who are married to people with similar religious orientations—76.6 percent for fundamentalists, 78.1 percent for moderates, and 73.4 percent for liberals. Thus, marriages are characterized by homogamy in current religious affiliation as well as in religious socialization.

Let's experiment with one last technique we can use with tables: **subsets**. We can use the subset function to limit the respondents who are included in the analysis. For example, let's see if people who do not consider themselves to be very religious still have marriages characterized by religious homogamy. *Press <ENTER>* twice to get ready to run a new table. Again, make **53** or **SP.FUND.** the row variable and **52** or **R.FUND/LIB** the column variable. *Press <ENTER>* to skip the control variable prompt. However, this time, when you are asked to enter the name or number of variable 1 for defining subset, *type* **50** or **HOW RELIG?** and *press <ENTER>*. The screen tells you that the low value on this variable is 1 and the high value is 3. *Press* **F3** to look at the variable description for **50) HOW RELIG?** (use the **page down** key to quickly move down the variable list). Once you have highlighted the variable, *press* the **right arrow** key. People who are somewhat committed to their religious denomination are in category 2 and those who are not very committed are in category 3. Therefore, *press <ENTER>* twice to close the variable description windows, *type* **2**, and *press <ENTER>* to set the lower limit at 2. Since those who say they are not very committed are in category 3, you want to make that your upper limit. So *type* **3** and *press <ENTER>*. When you are asked for the second subset variable, *press <ENTER>* to move on. The table appears on the screen. *Type* **C**.

	FUNDAMENT.	MODERATE	LIBERAL
FUNDAMENT.	63.7	9.2	9.9
MODERATE	21.0	73.6	19.3
LIBERAL	15.3	17.2	70.7

This table includes only those respondents who indicated that they are not very committed to their religious denomination (or only somewhat religious). Still, it demonstrates the influence of religious homogamy on mate selection. In this subgroup of less religious individuals, 63.7 percent of the fundamentalists are married to fundamentalists, 73.6 percent of the moderates are married to moderates, and 70.7 percent of the liberals are married to liberals. People tend to have homogamous marriages even on the basis of traits that they may not consider very important.

Based on the analyses presented thus far, we can conclude that with regard to age, education, and social upbringing, most marriages are homogamous. Although we are free to marry anyone whom we please, most people are attracted to those who are similar to themselves. There are many fish in the sea, but most of us choose to stay in our own ponds.

But what about those who marry people who are different from themselves—are those marriages any less likely to succeed? After a couple says "I do," does homogamy make a difference? To answer that question, let's take a look at the impact of homogamy and heterogamy on marital happiness in the following exercises.

NAME:

COURSE:

DATE:

Open the **NORC** data file and select the **Tabular Statistics** function.

1. The hypothesis is: **Spouses who have the same level of education will be more likely to rate their marriage as very happy.**

Make **59** or **HAPPY.MAR?** the row variable and **48** or **ED.HOMOGAM** the column variable, and use **1** or **SEX** as the control variable. *Press* **C** *(*for Column percentages). Fill in the first table for males.

MALES

	ED HETERO	ED HOMOG
LESS HAPPY	%	%
MORE HAPPY	%	%

Prob. = _____

V = _____

Is the difference statistically significant? (circle one)   Yes   No

Is the hypothesis supported or rejected? (circle one)   Supported   Rejected

Press <ENTER> until the results for females appear on the screen. (Make sure the label for females appears at the top left of the screen.) *Press* **C** (for Column percentages). Fill in the table below.

FEMALES

	ED HETERO	ED HOMOG
LESS HAPPY	%	%
MORE HAPPY	%	%

Prob. = _____

V = _____

Is the difference statistically significant? (circle one)   Yes   No

Is the hypothesis supported or rejected? (circle one)   Supported   Rejected

How would you explain the results of this analysis in relationship to the hypothesis?

2. The hypothesis is: **Married people who were socialized into similar religions will be more likely to rate their marriages as very happy.**

   Make **59** or **HAPPY.MAR?** the row variable and **57** or **R16HOMOG.** the column variable. *Press <ENTER>* once to skip the control variable option. When you are asked for a subset variable, use **50** or **HOW RELIG?**. Set the lower limit at 1 and the maximum value at 2. This means that those who consider themselves to be at least somewhat committed to their religious denomination will be included in the analysis. *Press* **C** (for Column percentages). Fill in the table.

	REL HETERO	REL HOMOG
LESS HAPPY	%	%
MORE HAPPY	%	%

   Prob. = _____

   V = _____

   Is the difference statistically significant? (circle one)   Yes   No

   Is the hypothesis supported or rejected? (circle one)   Supported   Rejected

   The hypothesis is: **Married people who share the same religious orientation will be more likely to rate their marriages as very happy.**

   Make **59** or **HAPPY.MAR?** the row variable and **56** or **REL HOMOG** the column variable. Again, use **50** or **HOW RELIG?** as the subset variable, with a minimum value of 1 and a maximum value of 2. *Press* **C** (for Column percentages). Fill in the table.

	REL HETERO	REL HOMOG
LESS HAPPY	%	%
MORE HAPPY	%	%

Prob. = _____

V = _____

Is the difference statistically significant? (circle one)   Yes   No

Is the hypothesis supported or rejected? (circle one)   Supported   Rejected

Based on the two preceding hypotheses, what can you conclude about the relationship between religious homogamy and marital happiness?

3. The hypothesis is: **Spouses who have the same level of education will have sex more frequently than couples with different levels of education.**

Make **60** or **FREQ.SEX** the row variable and **48** or **ED.HOMOGAM** the column variable *Press <ENTER>* to skip the control variable option. Let's limit our analysis to individuals who are under the age of 65. So select **2** or **AGE** as the subset variable and make 1 the lower limit and 4 the upper limit. *Press* **C** (for Column percentages). Fill in the table.

	ED HETERO	ED HOMOG
UNDER 3/YR	%	%
1 – 4 / MO	%	%
2 – 3 / WK	%	%

Prob. = _____

V = _____

Is the difference statistically significant? (circle one)   Yes   No

Is the hypothesis supported or rejected? (circle one)   Supported   Rejected

The hypothesis is: **Spouses who have similar religious orientations will have sex more frequently than couples with different religious orientations.**

Make **60** or **FREQ.SEX** the row variable and **56** or **REL HOMOG** the column variable. *Press <ENTER>* to skip the control variable option. Let's again limit our analysis to individuals who are under the age of 65. Make **2** or **AGE** the subset variable using 1 as the lower limit and 4 as the upper limit. *Press* **C** (for Column percentages). Fill in the table.

	REL HETERO	REL HOMOG
UNDER 3/YR	%	%
1 – 4 / MO	%	%
2 – 3 / WK	%	%

Prob. = _____

V = _____

Is the difference statistically significant? (circle one)   Yes   No

Is the hypothesis supported or rejected? (circle one)   Supported   Rejected

How would you explain the results of the two previous tables?

4. Make **48** or **ED.HOMOGAM** the row variable and **6** or **AGE WED** the column variable. *Press* **C** (for Column percentages). Fill in the table.

	18 OR UNDE	19–20	21–22	23–25	OVER 25
ED HETERO	%	%	%	%	%
ED HOMOG	%	%	%	%	%

Prob. = _____

V = _____

Is the difference statistically significant? (circle one)   Yes   No

Make **56** or **REL HOMOG** the row variable and **6** or **AGE WED** the column variable. *Press* **C** (for Column percentages). Fill in the table.

	18 OR UNDE	19–20	21–22	23–25	OVER 25
REL HETERO	%	%	%	%	%
REL HOMOG	%	%	%	%	%

Prob. = _____

V = _____

Is the difference statistically significant? (circle one)   Yes   No

Summarize the relationship between educational and religious homogamy and age at marriage.

5. Open the **NSC** data file and return to the **Tabular Statistics** task. The hypothesis is: **Children whose parents are close in age are more likely than children whose parents are not close in age to believe that their parents get along well with each other.**

Make **10** or **GET ALONG** the row variable and **8** or **AGE.HOMOG** the column variable. *Press* **C** (for Column percentages). Fill in the the table below.

	5 + YEARS	4 OR LESS
VERY WELL	%	%
LESS WELL	%	%

Prob. = _____

V = _____

Is the difference statistically significant? (circle one)   Yes   No

Is the hypothesis supported or rejected? (circle one)   Supported   Rejected

What do you believe is the connection between age differences and marital harmony?

6. Now it's time to test your own hypothesis. You can use either the NORC or the NSC data file. Remember, you can use **F3** to view and select variables, or you can consult the list of variables in the back of your book and type in the name or number of the variable you wish to select.

Write a hypothesis using one of the measures of homogamy introduced in this exercise as either the independent (cause) or dependent (effect) variable:

_____

_____

What is your dependent variable?   _____
(make this your row variable)

What is your independent variable?   _____
(make this your column variable)

Type **C** (for Column percentages). *Press* **P** (for Print). (**Note:** If your computer is not connected to a printer, or you have been instructed not to use the printer, skip these printing instructions. Instead, draw a table on a separate sheet of paper showing the final, percentaged results.) Attach a copy of the results.

Is the difference statistically significant? (circle one)   Yes   No

Is the hypothesis supported or rejected? (circle one)   Supported   Rejected

Discuss why you think your hypothesis was, or was not, supported.

◆ CHAPTER 6 ◆
Mobile Families and Communities

Industrialization has done more than simply change the type of work we do on a daily basis. The transition from an agrarian to an industrial society also affects the places where we live. In agrarian societies, people tend to stay close to their roots because they are dependent on the land for their survival. Even if land is available, most children will not find it practical to move far from home to start a farm of their own with no one to share the labor. The best economic opportunities are at home, or at least in the same community. In this setting, the *extended* family (grandparents, cousins, and so on) is a valuable source of both economic and social support. Tangible assets such as land or tools can be shared, along with intangible assets such as knowledge, companionship, or assistance with child care.

Industrialization dramatically alters the distribution of the population and thus affects the structure of the family as well. Industrialization is inevitably accompanied by urbanization. With industrialization, economic opportunities lie not at home but in the marketplace. As agriculture becomes more productive and less labor-intensive, the demand for workers shifts from the farm to the factory. Thus, young people begin looking to the city for their future.

The *nuclear* family, which consists of a married couple and any children they may have, is compatible with life in an industrialized, urbanized society. Extended family ties may be a hindrance to economic and social opportunity if they keep one from pursuing other possibilities. The reduction of responsibilities to the extended family allows children freedom to move away when they get old enough to pursue their own interests, such as going to college or taking a job in another state. Sociologist William Goode described the relationship between an industrialized society and nuclear families as being a *good fit*.[1] The economy benefits by having a trained and mobile work force, while individuals benefit from increased personal freedom. However, Goode also warns that isolation from the resources of the extended family can produce both economic and social hardships as nuclear families are asked to take on more responsibilities than they can bear.

What are families like in the contemporary U.S.? Are they more extended or nuclear? Most social scientists would say that in the U.S. we have *relatively* isolated nuclear families. Although the emphasis is on the nuclear family, most people are not completely isolated from their extended families, whether by choice or by necessity. The purpose of this exercise will be to take a closer look at the geographic mobility of American families and the impact that mobility has on local communities.

Open the **NORC** data file and go to **A. Univariate Statistics**. When you are asked for the name or number of the variable you wish to examine, *type* **27** or **SOC.KIN** and *press <ENTER>*. *Press <ENTER>* again to skip the subset option.

---

[1] William Goode, 1964. *The Family*. Englewood Cliffs, N.J.: Prentice-Hall.

HOW OFTEN: Spend a social evening with relatives?

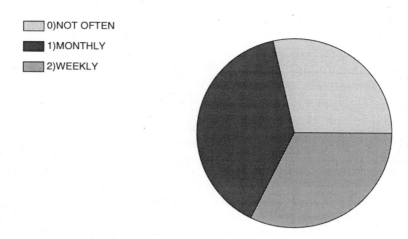

☐ 0)NOT OFTEN
■ 1)MONTHLY
▨ 2)WEEKLY

This graph shows how often people say they spend an evening socializing with relatives. *Press* **D** (for Distribution). The smallest category is those who say they do not socialize with relatives very often (28.7 percent). On the other hand, 32.3 percent say they socialize with family at least once per week, and an additional 39.1 percent socialize with family at least once per month. So it is safe to say that most people still believe that it is important to spend time with the extended family.

The one factor that probably inhibits socialization with kin more than any other is geographic mobility. Take a look at just how mobile we are in modern society. *Press <ENTER>* twice to clear the screen for another variable. This time, *type* **29** or **MOVERS** and *press <ENTER>* twice.

When you were 16 years old, were you living in the same (city/town/county)?

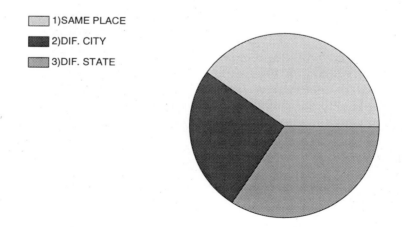

▨ 1)SAME PLACE
■ 2)DIF. CITY
▨ 3)DIF. STATE

Press **D** (for Distribution). Less than half (40.1 percent) of the respondents live in the same place where they were born, 25.7 percent live in a different city, and 34.1 percent live in a different state. So how does this mobility affect how often people socialize with extended family? *Press <ENTER>* three times to return to the **STATISTICAL ANALYSIS MENU**. Move the highlight to **B. Tabular Statistics** and *press <ENTER>*. When you are asked for the name or number of the row variable, *type* **27** or **SOC.KIN** and *press <ENTER>*. When you are asked for the name or number of the column variable, *type* **29** or **MOVERS** and keep *pressing <ENTER>* until the table appears on your screen. *Type* **C** (for Column percentages).

	SAME PLACE	DIF. CITY	DIF. STATE
NOT OFTEN	18.9	24.9	44.7
MONTHLY	40.0	47.1	30.9
WEEKLY	41.1	28.0	24.4

Does geographic mobility affect how much we interact with extended family? It certainly does. Reading across the bottom category, among those who live in the same place where they were born, 41.1 percent visit with relatives at least once a week, by comparison with 28 percent for those who have moved to a different city and 24.4 percent for those who have moved to a different state. The fact that only a handful of people say they never visit with relatives, even among those who have moved out of state, tells us that lack of socialization with relatives probably has more to do with time and geographic constraints than with the quality of the relationships.

Earlier, we suggested that people move away to pursue personal goals, such as getting an education. Let's see if we can back that up. The hypothesis is: **College graduates will be more likely to have moved out of state.** *Press <ENTER>* to clear the screen for a new table. This time, use **29** or **MOVERS** as the row variable and **42** or **DEGREE** as the column variable. When the table appears on your screen, *press* **C** (for Column percentages). Here are the results:

	NOT H.S.	HIGH SCH.	JR. COL.	B.A.	GRAD. DEG.
SAME PLACE	51.0	44.0	38.1	25.5	20.7
DIF. CITY	21.5	26.2	30.0	27.3	25.1
DIF. STATE	27.5	29.8	31.9	47.2	54.2

Reading across the bottom row, we see that the more education one has, the more likely one is to move out of state. The biggest jump is between the category for junior college graduates (31.9 percent) and graduates of four-year colleges (47.2 percent). *Press* **S** (for Statistics). The results are statistically significant (Prob. = 0.000). The hypothesis is supported; getting a college education reduces the likelihood that you will remain close to your roots.

If geographic mobility is a response to the demands of an industrialized society, moving away from one's family is less a matter of personal choice than it is a by-product of modern life. So let's switch to the ecological data to see what this geographic mobility looks like from a more distant perspective.

Open the **STATES** data file and return to the **STATISTICAL ANALYSIS MENU**. Place the highlight on **E. Mapping Variables** and *press <ENTER>*. This data set contains several indicators of geographic mobility. We can begin by looking at the percentage of the population who have not moved from the state in which they were born. To look at that variable, *type* **6** or **NO MOVE** and *press <ENTER>*. This map will appear:

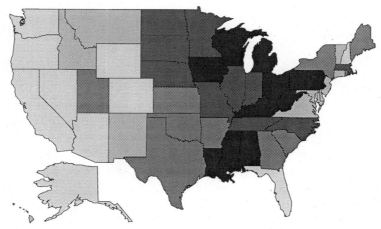

1990: Percent Born in State of Residence

The highest concentration of nonmovers is in the central and south central portions of the U.S. *Type* **D** (for Distribution). Pennsylvania has the most geographically stable population, with 80.2 percent having been born there, followed by Louisiana and Iowa. The most mobile population lives in Nevada, where only 21.8 percent of the residents are native to the state.

In the survey data, we found that geographic mobility was related to education; let's see if we can replicate those findings with ecological data. *Press <ENTER>* several times until you return to the main menu. Select **F. Scatterplots** and make **6** or **NO MOVE** the dependent variable and **53** or **% COLLEGE** the independent variable. *Press <ENTER>* to skip the subset option. When the scatterplot appears, *press* **L** to view the regression line. The downward slope and the negative correlation (r = −.42) tell us that as the percentage of residents who are college graduates increases, the percentage of residents who have lived in the state all their lives decreases. An educated population is geographically mobile. This finding supports the results of the analysis using the survey data.

Once people have received an education, they could return to their hometowns, but those may not be where the good jobs are located. In a society where families have free choice, we would expect most people to move to areas where jobs are available and pay well. If that is the case, then **states where the population is growing will be more urban and have higher incomes**. Return to the **STATISTICAL ANALYSIS MENU** and select **G. Correlation**. Enter **5** or **POP GO 90** as the first variable, followed by **9** or **%URBAN** and **45** or **MED.FAM $**. *Press <ENTER>* two more times to see the final table.

	5) POP GO 90	9) %URBAN	45) MED.FAM $
5) POP GO 90	—	0.417**	0.304*
9) %URBAN	0.417**	—	0.570**
45) MED.FAM $	0.304*	0.570**	—

Variable **5) POP GO 90** is the percent growth (or decline) of a state's population between 1980 and 1990. As expected, people are moving to areas that are more urban (r = 0.417) because that is where the jobs are, as well as the higher median family incomes (r = 0.304). Again, moving away from one's family has less to do with the quality of family relationships than it does with the availability of economic opportunities. In a society where nuclear families are free to decide where to live, they will choose more affluent, urban areas—even if that means moving out of state.

Is the mobility of the population today increasing, or has there been a leveling off now that most people are no longer born in rural areas? One way we can answer that question is by looking at the relationship between age and geographic mobility. *Press <ENTER> to clear the screen for a new list of variables.* This time, use **6** or **NO MOVE**, **15** or **% OVER 65**, and **12** or **% UNDER 5**. *Press <ENTER> twice.*

	6) NO MOVE	15) % OVER 65	12) % UNDER 5
6) NO MOVE	—	0.327**	−0.317*
15) % OVER 65	0.327**	—	−0.770**
12) % UNDER 5	−0.317*	−0.770**	—

Variable **6) NO MOVE** is the percent of residents who live in the state where they were born. Here we see that states with a higher percentage of native-born residents tend to have more persons aged 65 or older (r = .327), and fewer children under the age of 5 (r = −.317). So, it is the younger families who are the most mobile in our society. Even though most people are now born in urban areas with at least some access to education and a variety of occupations, the movement away from our hometowns continues.

Today, most people take the freedom to move away from one's family in order to pursue individual goals for granted—but what effect does this geographic mobility have on society as a whole? When people live in one area for a long time, they are more likely to be integrated into the community through family, friendships, and membership in community organizations. Does it make a difference that people are no longer as integrated into their communities as generations may have been in the past? In the exercises that follow, your attention will be directed to some other societal factors that may be related to geographic mobility. In some cases, you may believe the relationships are cause-and-effect. Other relationships you may associate with factors not related to mobility. Either way, it is clear that our geographically mobile families are part of a broader social fabric in which everything is connected.

WORKSHEET

NAME: _____

COURSE: _____

DATE: _____

Workbook exercises and software are copyrighted. Copying is prohibited by law.

EXERCISE

6

1. Open the **STATES** data file and select the **Scatterplot** function. Create the following scatterplot, using population growth as an indicator of social integration:

   Dependent variable: **61** or **CH.MEMBER**

   Independent variable: **5** or **POP GO 90**

   What is the correlation coefficient?   r = _____

   Is the correlation statistically significant? (circle one)   Yes   No

   How would you explain the relationship between the population growth rate and church membership?

2. Create the following scatterplot:

   Dependent variable: **65** or **SUICIDE**

   Independent variable: **6** or **NO MOVE**

   What is the correlation coefficient?   r = _____

   Is the correlation statistically significant? (circle one)   Yes   No

   Do you think this is a cause-and-effect relationship? Explain. (Remember, to view the variable descriptions, select **X** or **Y** from the bottom menu.)

3. *Press <ENTER>* twice to return to the **STATISTICAL ANALYSIS MENU**. Select **G. Correlation**. Use the following list of variables to fill in the table below: **6) NO MOVE, 20) % WHITE**, and **21) % BLACK**.

	6) NO MOVE	20) % WHITE	21) % BLACK
6) NO MOVE			
20) % WHITE			
21) % BLACK			

What is the correlation between **% WHITE** and geographic mobility? _____

Is the correlation statistically significant? (circle one)   Yes   No

What is the correlation between **% BLACK** and geographic mobility? _____

Is the correlation statistically significant? (circle one)   Yes   No

How would you describe the relationship between race and geographic mobility?

4. Use the following list of variables to fill in the table below: **6) NO MOVE, 67) P.CRIME**, and **68) V.CRIME**.

	6) NO MOVE	67) P.CRIME	68) V.CRIME
6) NO MOVE			
67) P.CRIME			
68) V.CRIME			

What is the correlation between property crime and geographic mobility? _____

Is the correlation statistically significant? (circle one)   Yes   No

What is the correlation between violent crime and geographic mobility? _____

Is the correlation statistically significant? (circle one)   Yes   No

How would you explain the difference between these two types of crime and geographic mobility?

5. *Press <ENTER>* to clear the screen for a new list of variables. This time, you can select your own dependent variables. When you are asked for the first variable, *type* **6** or **NO MOVE**. Then select a second variable that you think will be related to geographic mobility. (**Reminder:** You can use **F3** to see a list of the variables, or you can consult the list of variables in the back of your book and type in the name or number of the variable you wish to select.)

Which variable did you select? _____

Write a hypothesis using **6) NO MOVE** as the independent variable and the variable you selected as the dependent variable:

_____

_____

What is the correlation coefficient? r = _____

Is the correlation statistically significant? (circle one) Yes No

Is your hypothesis supported or rejected? (circle one) Supported Rejected

Press **P** (for Print). (**Note:** If your computer is not connected to a printer, or if you have been instructed not to use the printer, skip these printing instructions. Instead, draw a table on a separate sheet of paper showing the final results.) Attach a copy of your results.

Explain why you think your hypothesis was or was not supported.

CHAPTER 7

Gender Roles

Although the terms *sex* and *gender* are commonly used interchangeably, social scientists make a distinction between these two concepts. *Sex* refers to the *biological* characteristic of being female or male. *Gender* refers to *masculinity* and *femininity*—the *social* characteristics associated with being male or female. For example, most cultures associate aggression with the male sex and nurturing with the female sex. When definitions of masculinity or femininity become associated with specific social responsibilities, social scientists refer to those as *gender roles*. Women, for instance, have been expected to assume most of the responsibility for child care because nurturing has been seen as a female trait. Men have traditionally been expected to put their energies into protecting and providing for the family.

Because gender roles are socially defined, they change as the society changes. For example, less than a century ago, education was primarily considered a masculine pursuit and most women did not even have the option of attending college. Today, a majority of college students are female.

The area of social change that has received the most attention is the movement of women into the paid labor force. Although women have always shared in providing for the physical needs of the family, the shift from working in the home to working in the paid labor force is a major social change. In this chapter, we will examine some of the attitudes and actions associated with this social change.

Start MicroCase, open the **NORC** data file, and go to the **Tabular Statistics** function. When you are asked for the name or number of the row variable, *type* **39** or **WOMEN WORK** and *press* *<ENTER>*. When you are prompted for the name or number of the column variable, *type* **1** or **SEX** and *press* *<ENTER>*. *Press <ENTER>* twice and *press* **C** (for Column percentages). These results will appear:

	MALE	FEMALE
APPROVE	81.0	80.8
DISAPPROVE	19.0	19.2

The vast majority of both men (81 percent) and women (80.8 percent) approve of women in the work force. Does this mean that with regard to gender roles there is equality between the sexes, or are people just answering this question in a way that seems socially acceptable? Let's look at some more detailed questions that will help us make this distinction. *Press <ENTER>* once to clear the screen for a new table.

Type **40** or **HELP HUBBY** as the name or number for the row variable and *press* *<ENTER>*. *Type* **1** or **SEX** as the column variable and *press* *<ENTER>*. *Press <ENTER>* twice and *press* **C** (for Column percentages). This question asks respondents whether they agree with the statement that it is more important for a wife to help her husband's career than to have one herself. Here is what your results look like:

	MALE	FEMALE
STR.AGREE	2.9	3.3
AGREE	20.1	18.5
DISAGREE	60.6	51.7
STR.DISAG	16.4	26.5

Only a small percentage of men (2.9 percent) and women (3.3 percent) *strongly agree* that a woman should support her husband's career rather than pursue one of her own. The most noticeable distinction between the two groups is in the *strongly disagree* response. Women (26.5 percent) are much more likely than men (16.4 percent) to strongly disagree with the idea that a wife should put her husband's career before her own. *Press* **S** (for Statistics). Prob. = 0.000, so the difference is statistically significant. Women are less likely to believe that their husbands' careers are more important than their own.

Let's look at one more measure of gender role attitudes. *Press <ENTER>* twice to clear the screen for a new table. This time, select **41** or **STAY HOME** as the row variable and **1** or **SEX** as the column variable. Make sure to use column percentaging when the final table appears. The question **STAY HOME** asks respondents whether they agree with the statement "It is much better for everyone involved if the man is the achiever outside the home and the woman takes care of the home and family." These are the results:

	MALE	FEMALE
STR.AGREE	6.6	6.5
AGREE	32.1	26.5
DISAGREE	48.5	45.4
STR.DISAG	12.7	21.6

The results in this table are quite similar to those in the previous table. About the same percentage of men (6.6 percent) and women (6.5 percent) strongly agree with the notion that it is best for everyone if a mother does not work outside the home. Again, the most noticeable difference is in the *strongly disagree* response. Men (12.7 percent) are less likely than women (21.6 percent) to disagree with the idea that it is generally best for all concerned if a wife does not work outside the home. *Press* **S** and you'll see that the difference here also is statistically significant (Prob. = 0.000). While both sexes are generally supportive of women's working outside the home, women are generally more committed to this principle than are men.

One of the easiest ways to observe how gender roles have changed over time is by comparing different age groups. If gender roles are changing over time, we can expect the following hypothesis to be supported: **Younger people will be more likely than older people to approve of married women working outside the home.** *Press <ENTER>* twice to clear the screen for a new table. This time, use **39** or **WOMEN WORK** as the row variable and **2** or **AGE** as the column variable. Make sure to use column percentaging for the final results.

	18–29	30–39	40–49	50–64	65 & OVER
APPROVE	86.8	84.1	83.0	79.5	69.6
DISAPPROVE	13.2	15.9	17.0	20.5	30.4

The results are consistent with the hypothesis; as age goes up, the percentage of people who approve of a woman's working outside the home declines. Although a majority of those in each age category do approve of women's working outside the home, those aged 18 to 29 are the most likely to approve of women's working outside the home (86.8 percent) while those aged 65 or older are the least likely to approve (69.6 percent). *Press* **S** (for Statistics). Prob. = 0.000, so the difference is statistically significant. The hypothesis is supported: younger people do have less traditional gender role attitudes.

Another comparison we can look for is between those who attend church and those who do not. Let's test this hypothesis: **People who attend church regularly will be less likely to approve of married women's working outside the home.** Select **39** or **WOMEN WORK** as the row variable and **49** or **CH.ATTEND** as the column variable. Use column percentaging for the final results. This table will appear:

	LESS OFTEN	ANNUALLY	MONTHLY	WEEKLY
APPROVE	83.1	82.5	80.8	78.1
DISAPPROVE	16.9	17.5	19.2	21.9

The results are somewhat consistent with the hypothesis—there is a pattern indicating that the more people attend church, the less likely they are to approve of married women's working outside the home. But the differences are not very great. Among those who attend church less than once a year, 83.1 percent approve of married women's being employed, as compared to 78.1 for those who attend church weekly. *Press* **S** (for Statistics). The difference is statistically significant (Prob. = 0.044), but the differences are so small that they lack any substantive significance.

Perhaps we need to take into consideration the tendency of some churches to be more accepting of social change than others. Try using **39** or **WOMEN WORK** again as the row variable, only this time, use **52** or **R.FUND/LIB** as the column variable. Remember to use column percentaging. Here are the results:

	FUNDAMENT.	MODERATE	LIBERAL
APPROVE	76.5	81.6	84.8
DISAPPROVE	23.5	18.4	15.2

You might recall from an earlier exercise that **R.FUND/LIB** indicates how fundamental or liberal the church denomination is (for those who attend church). The trend here is slightly more distinct than the previous example. Religious fundamentalists (76.5 percent) are less approving than either religious moderates (81.6 percent) or liberals (84.8 percent) of women in the work force. A look at the statistics reveals that the differences are statistically significant (Prob. = 0.000). Still, regardless of their religious orientation, most people approve of married women's working outside the home.

Education is another factor that is generally associated with changing gender role attitudes. Because college students are encouraged to critically evaluate traditional social norms, we would expect that **people who attend college will be more likely to approve of married women's working outside the home.** Use **39** or **WOMEN WORK** as the row variable and **42** or **DEGREE** as the column variable to get these percentaged results:

	NOT H.S.	HIGH SCH.	JR. COL.	B.A.	GRAD. DEG.
APPROVE	68.9	81.2	81.8	87.8	89.9
DISAPPROVE	31.1	18.8	18.2	12.2	10.1

As expected, the more educated people are, the more likely they are to approve of nontraditional gender roles. Those with less than a high school degree are the least likely to approve of a woman's working outside the home (68.9 percent) while those with a graduate degree are the most likely to approve (89.9 percent). *Press* **S** (for Statistics). The results are statistically significant (Prob. = 0.000). The hypothesis is supported.

Let's shift from looking at attitudes to looking at actions. Return to the main menu and go to the **Univariate Statistics** function. Select **33** or **MAR.F.WRK**, which is short for *married women's work status. Press <ENTER>* to skip the subset variable option. Married women who are retired or are full-time students are not included in this sample. When the pie chart appears, *press* **D** (for Distribution). Here is the distribution you will see:

	FREQUENCY	%
FULL TIME	553	51.2
PART TIME	180	16.7
HOMEMAKER	347	32.1

The majority of married women in this sample are employed full-time outside the home, and a sizable proportion of the rest are employed at least part-time. Approximately one third of the women surveyed consider themselves to be full-time homemakers. In the exercises that follow, you will have the opportunity to examine some of the differences between the women in each of these three groups.

Your turn.

NAME:

COURSE:

DATE:

Open the **NORC** data file and select the **Tabular Statistics** function.

1. The hypothesis is: **Women who attend fundamentalist churches will be less likely than those who attend moderate or liberal churches to be employed full-time.**

   Make **33** or **MAR.F.WRK** the row variable and **52** or **R.FUND/LIB** the column variable. *Press* **C** (for Column percentages). Fill in the table.

	FUNDAMENT.	MODERATE	LIBERAL
FULL TIME	%	%	%
PART TIME	%	%	%
HOMEMAKER	%	%	%

Prob. = _____

V = _____

Is the difference statistically significant? (circle one)　　　　　　Yes　　No

Is the hypothesis supported or rejected? (circle one)　　　Supported　　Rejected

How would you explain these results?

2. The hypothesis is: **Women with more education will be more likely to be employed full-time.**

Make **33** or **MAR.F.WRK** the row variable and **42** or **DEGREE** the column variable. *Press* **C** (for Column percentages). Fill in the table.

	NOT H.S.	HIGH SCH.	JR. COL.	B.A.	GRAD. DEG.
FULL TIME	%	%	%	%	%
PART TIME	%	%	%	%	%
HOMEMAKER	%	%	%	%	%

Prob. = _____

V = _____

Is the difference statistically significant? (circle one)   Yes   No

Is the hypothesis supported or rejected? (circle one)   Supported   Rejected

How would you explain these results?

3. Create and fill in the table below. For the row variable use **33** or **MAR.F.WRK**. For the column variable use **3** or **WH/BLACK**. *Press* **C** (for Column percentages).

	WHITE	BLACK
FULL TIME	%	%
PART TIME	%	%
HOMEMAKER	%	%

Prob. = _____

V = _____

Is the difference statistically significant? (circle one)   Yes   No

Create and fill in the table below. For the row variable use **42** or **DEGREE**. For the column variable use **3** or **WH/BLACK**. *Press <ENTER>* once to skip the control variable option. When you are asked for a subset, select **1** or **SEX**. Set both the lower limit and the upper limit to 2 (this limits the analysis to only females) and *press <ENTER>* to view the final table. Now *press* **C** (for Column percentages).

	WHITE	BLACK
NOT H.S.	%	%
HIGH SCH.	%	%
JR. COL.	%	%
B.A.	%	%
GRAD.DEG.	%	%

Prob. = _____

V = _____

Is the difference statistically significant? (circle one)   Yes   No

Are these findings consistent with your explanation of the results from the previous question? How would you describe the relationship between race and the work status of married women?

4.   Create and fill in the table below. Make **33** or **MAR.F.WRK** the row variable and **13** or **# CHILDREN** the column variable. *Press* **C** (for Column percentages).

	NONE	1 – 2	3 OR MORE
FULL TIME	%	%	%
PART TIME	%	%	%
HOMEMAKER	%	%	%

Prob. = _____

V = _____

Is the difference statistically significant? (circle one)   Yes   No

Which of these variables do you believe is the independent variable? That is, do women have more children because they are not employed, or are they not employed because they have more children? Explain your answer.

5. Use **F3** to view the complete description for **59) HAPPY.MAR?**. Now make **59** or **HAPPY.MAR?** the row variable and **33** or **MAR.F.WRK** the column variable. *Press* **C** (for Column percentages). Fill in the table below.

	FULL TIME	PART TIME	HOMEMAKER
LESS HAPPY	%	%	%
VERY HAPPY	%	%	%

Prob. = _____

V = _____

Is the difference statistically significant? (circle one)   Yes   No

Summarize the results of this table in one or two sentences. Then explain why you think these results occur.

6. Question **35) INC.IMP** asks respondents if having a high income is one of the most important things in life. Make **35** or **INC.IMP** the row variable and **1** or **SEX** the column variable. Skip the control variable option by *pressing <ENTER>* once. Let's limit this analysis to only those individuals who are married. So when you are asked for a subset, select **4** or **MARITAL**, with a minimum value of 1 and a maximum value of 1. Let's further limit the analysis to only those individuals who work full-time. So when asked for a second subset variable, select **32** or **WORK STAT**, with a minimum value of 1 and a maximum value of 1. *Press* **C** (for Column percentages). These results compare males or females (who are married and working full-time) on whether they think that a high income is one of the most important things in life. Fill in the table.

	MALE	FEMALE
MOST IMP.	%	%
NOT MOST	%	%

Prob. = _____

V = _____

Is the difference statistically significant? (circle one)   Yes   No

Question **36) ACCOM.IMP** asks respondents how important it is that work gives you a feeling of accomplishment. This time make **36** or **ACCOM.IMP** the row variable and **1** or **SEX** the column variable. *Press <ENTER>* once to skip the control variable option. Let's again limit the analysis to those who are married and who work full-time. So when you are asked for a subset, select **4** or **MARITAL**, with a minimum value of 1 and a maximum value of 1. When you are asked for a second subset variable, select **32** or **WORK STAT**, with a minimum value of 1 and a maximum value of 1. *Press* **C** (for Column percentages). Fill in the table.

	MALE	FEMALE
MOST IMP.	%	%
NOT MOST	%	%

Prob. = _____

V = _____

Is the difference statistically significant? (circle one)   Yes   No

Summarize the last two tables and give an explanation for the results.

7. Now it's time to test your own hypothesis. Remember, you can use **F3** to view and select variables, or you can consult the list of variables in the back of your book and type in the name or number of the variable you wish to select.

Write a hypothesis using **33** or **MAR.F.WRK** as either the independent (cause) or dependent (effect) variable:

_____

_____

What is your dependent variable?   _____
(make this your row variable)

What is your independent variable?   _____
(make this your column variable)

Type **C** (for Column percentages). *Press* **P** (for Print). (**Note:** If your computer is not connected to a printer, or you have been instructed not to use the printer, skip these printing instructions. Instead, draw a table on a separate sheet of paper showing the final, percentaged results.) Attach a copy of the results.

Is the difference statistically significant? (circle one)   Yes   No

Is the hypothesis supported or rejected? (circle one)   Supported   Rejected

Discuss the reasons why you think your hypothesis was, or was not, supported.

CHAPTER 8

Female Employment, 1920–1990

Although the concept of *going* to work is taken for granted today, it is a relatively recent phenomenon when viewed in historical context. For thousands of years prior to industrialization, both men and women participated in the provision of food, shelter, and clothing for the family—and most of this production took place *in* the home. There was no discussion about women, or for that matter men, working outside the home—because most of the work to be done was done at home.

During the past 300 years, production has gradually moved from the home to economic institutions that are distinct and separate from the family. In an industrialized society, going to work generally means being away from the family. This puts families in the relatively new position of deciding who should go to work—the husband, the wife, or both? Of course, one need not be employed to be involved in economic production. Persons who are not employed may still be involved in maintaining the home and producing goods and services for their families and others. But the question of how husbands and wives should divide the responsibilities for paid employment still remains.

Most of the debate surrounding family sex roles has centered on the role of women. It was generally accepted as *natural* that men would leave their homes to provide for their families, but that women would not. Women have had to balance their desire to be employed, or the economic necessity of employment, against a cultural expectation that their primary responsibility is to nurture their families. Today, a majority of women are employed. But, as we will see in this exercise, women's rates of participation in the paid labor force, and the impact of that participation on the family, have varied dramatically throughout the past century.[1]

Open the **STATES** data file and go to the **STATISTICAL ANALYSIS MENU**. Place the highlight on **E. Mapping Variables** and *press <ENTER>*. Now you are asked for the name or number of the variable you wish to map. *Type* **49** or *%***FEM.WRK90** and *press <ENTER>*.

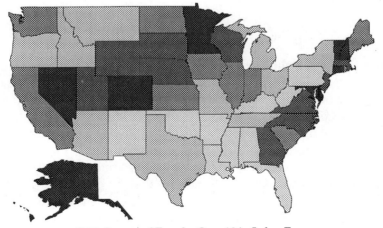

1990: Percent of Females Over 16 in Labor Force

---

[1] Portions of this exercise are based on presentations developed by Rodney Stark and published in *Family and Socialization in North America*, MicroCase Corporation, 1987.

This map shows female employment rates for 1990—the percentage of women aged 16 and over who are in the paid labor force. You will see that female employment rates are not highly regional, except that the rates are lower in the South. *Type* **D** (for Distribution). The state with the largest percentage of employed women is Alaska (66.42 percent), followed by New Hampshire (64.44 percent) and Maryland (63.36 percent). West Virginia has the lowest female employment rate (42.63 percent) and is the only state where less than half the female population is employed. In all, 7 of the 10 states with the lowest female employment rates are in the South.

Now let's go back to 1920. *Press <ENTER>* twice. When you are asked for the name or number of the variable you wish to map, *type* **95** or **%FEM.WRK20** and *press <ENTER>*.

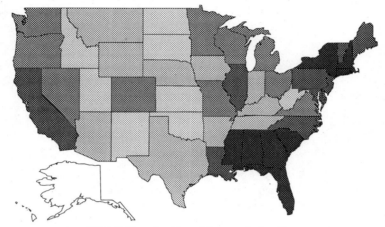

1920: % Females 16 and Over in Labor Force

The picture here is very different. *Type* **D** (for Distribution). First, you will notice that in no state are a majority of the women employed. South Carolina's female employment rate of 37 percent was the highest of that time. This draws our attention to the second trend: Whereas in 1990 female employment is lowest in the South, in 1920 that was where many of the states with the highest rates were located. In addition to South Carolina, Mississippi (31.7 percent), Georgia (29.8 percent), Alabama (27.8 percent), and Florida (27.1 percent) are all among the 10 states with the highest female employment rates. The rest of the top 10 states are located in the Northeast.

Part of the explanation for the shifting female employment rates in the South can be found by comparing the *reasons* women used to take jobs outside the home with the reasons many women are employed today. But this is best explained if we take a step back even further—to the 1880s. In 1880, just after the abolition of slavery, under 15 percent of American women held jobs outside the home. This picture changed dramatically in the South over the following decades. As was shown above, employment rates in southern states more than doubled by the 1920s. But the fact is, one of every five working women in the U.S. was African American in 1920, while only one of every ten women was African American. Or, put another way, in 1920, 44 percent of African American women worked—not far behind the current rate today—while only 20 percent of native-born white women worked outside the home.

Let's return to our question: Why do women take jobs outside the home? *Press <ENTER>* three times to return to the **STATISTICAL ANALYSIS MENU**. Switch to **F. Scatterplots**. When you are asked for the name or number of the dependent variable, *type* **95** or **%FEM.WRK20** and *press <ENTER>*. When you are asked for the name or number of the independent variable, *type* **94** or

Marriage and Family

F WAGES 20 and *press <ENTER>* twice. When the scatterplot appears, *type* **L** to view the regression line.

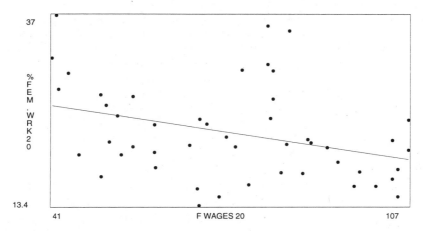

This scatterplot shows a negative correlation (r = −.344) between what was paid to a farm hand in 1920 and the female employment rate in 1920. In 1920, a large proportion of men who earned wages outside the home were employed as farm hands. So farm wages is a good indicator of the typical income that many men brought home from work. As we can see from the scatterplot, more women worked in states where the farm wages were lower. This would suggest that in 1920 many of the women who were employed were working only out of dire economic necessity—that is, their husbands did not make sufficient income to support the family.

Let's move 20 years closer to the present and look at 1940. *Press <ENTER>* to clear the screen for a new scatterplot. This time, use **91** or **%FEM.WRK40** as the dependent variable and **92** or **MEDIAN$ 40** as the independent variable. When the scatterplot appears, *type* **L** (for regression Line). The scatterplot will look like this:

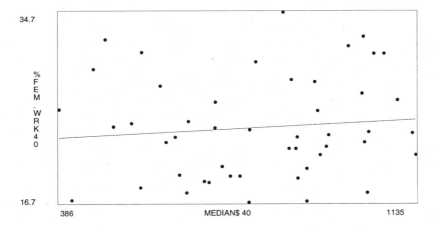

There is virtually no relationship between the female employment rate and the median income in 1940. The correlation of .098 is not statistically significant (Prob. = 0.254). Reasons for women's being employed other than family need appear to be emerging. Now let's take a look at more recent data to see if this shift is evidence of a trend. *Press <ENTER>* to clear the screen.

Select **49** or **%FEM.WRK90** as the dependent variable and **45** or **MED.FAM $** as the independent variable. When the scatterplot appears, *type* **L** (for regression Line):

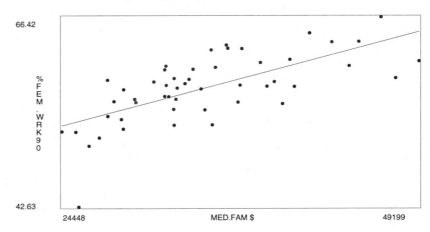

The results of this scatterplot are much more distinct and contrast starkly with the earlier findings. *There is a strong positive correlation (r = 0.685) between the female employment rate and the median family income in 1990.* In other words, whereas high female employment rates used to be associated with economic hardship, today high female employment rates are indicative of economic opportunity. In the past, upper-income families were overwhelmingly families in which the wives were not employed. Today, they are *primarily* two-earner families.

How can we account for this change in the relationship between economic need and female employment rates? Part of the explanation is economic. In the past, men and women could secure well-paying jobs even if they did not have a great deal of formal training, but that is no longer the case. More than ever before, education and economic opportunity are closely linked. Women who are married to men with lower incomes probably have a lower earning potential themselves. Many women's earnings may not even be enough to offset the cost of child care. In contrast, women who are married to upper-income men probably have more education and more attractive job opportunities themselves, which makes employment more attractive. Thus, the better off a woman is financially, the more likely she is to be employed.

But is this shift in women's employment patterns entirely economic, or is there an ideological component as well? Let's take a look at the way the female employment rate in 1990 is related to some other indicators of social thought—specifically feminism. One way to look for changes in attitudes toward women in the workplace is to look for the presence of women in traditionally male occupations. Being a physician and serving in the military are two such positions. *Press <ENTER> until you return to the* **STATISTICAL ANALYSIS MENU**. *Select* **G. Correlation**. *Enter each of the following variables:* **49** or **%FEM.WRK90**, **77** or **%FEM MD**, *and* **78** or **%FEM VET**. *Press <ENTER> to skip the subset option.*

	49) %FEM.WRK90	77) %FEM MD	78) %FEM VET
49) %FEM.WRK90	—	0.195	0.481**
77) %FEM MD	0.195	—	−0.012
78) %FEM VET	0.481**	−0.012	—

Reading down the first column, we can see how the variables listed are related to the female employment rate. The relationship between the female employment rate and the percentage of female M.D.s is not statistically significant (r = 0.195). However, there is a significant relationship between the female employment rate and the percentage of females who are military veterans (r = 0.481**). Thus, the gender barriers may be easier to overcome in some occupations than in others.

Another way to explore regional variations in sex-role attitudes is by looking at the distribution of *Ms.*, a magazine that is supportive of equal opportunities for women in the workplace. Let's use correlations to test the hypothesis that **states with more females in the work force will have more subscribers to *Ms.* magazine.** *Press <ENTER>* to clear the screen for a new list of variables. This time, use **49** or **%FEM.WRK90** and **86** or **MS**. *Press <ENTER>* to skip the subset option.

	49) %FEM.WRK90	86) MS.
49) %FEM.WRK90	—	0.576**
86) MS.	0.576**	—

The popularity of *Ms.* magazine may be somewhat speculative as a measure of feminism, but see how nicely it works? Where women read *Ms.*, they are also more likely to be employed (r = 0.576). The two asterisks next to the correlation tell us that the relationship is statistically significant at the 0.01 level. Because the correlation is in the predicted direction (positive) and because the relationship is statistically significant, we can say the hypothesis is supported. Based on all of these analyses, we can conclude that the female employment rate is associated with both economic and ideological factors.

Your turn.

WORKSHEET

NAME:

COURSE:

DATE:

EXERCISE

8

1. Open the **STATES** data file and select the scatterplot function. Create the following scatterplot:

   Dependent variable: **44** or **ABORTION**

   Independent variable: **49** or **%FEM.WRK90**

   What is the correlation coefficient?   r = _____

   Is the correlation statistically significant? (circle one)   Yes   No

   Describe the relationship between the female employment rate and abortion. How might you explain these results?

2. Create the following scatterplot:

   Dependent variable: **49** or **%FEM.WRK90**

   Independent variable: **53** or **% COLLEGE**

   What is the correlation coefficient?   r = _____

   Is the correlation statistically significant? (circle one)   Yes   No

   How would you explain this particular outcome?

3. The hypothesis is: **States with more females in the work force will have more people who voted for Bill Clinton in 1992.** Create the following scatterplot:

    Dependent variable: **74** or **%CLINTON92**

    Independent variable: **49** or **%FEM.WRK90**

    What is the correlation coefficient?   r = _____

    Is the correlation statistically significant? (circle one)   Yes   No

    Is the hypothesis supported or rejected? (circle one)   Supported   Rejected

    Were these the results you expected? Explain.

4. Create the following scatterplot:

    Dependent variable: **49** or **%FEM.WRK90**

    Independent variable: **27** or **%SINGLE F**

    What is the correlation coefficient?   r = _____

    Is the correlation statistically significant? (circle one)   Yes   No

    Create the following scatterplot:

    Dependent variable: **49** or **%FEM.WRK90**

    Independent variable: **34** or **%F.DIVORCE**

    What is the correlation coefficient?   r = _____

    Is the correlation statistically significant? (circle one)   Yes   No

Which has the greatest influence on the female employment rate—the proportion of single females or the proportion of divorced females? Why might these results occur?

5. *Press <ENTER>* twice to return to the **STATISTICAL ANALYSIS MENU**. Select **G. Correlation**. Use the following variables to fill in the table below: **49** or **%FEM.WRK90**, **64** or **% BAPTIST**, **63** or **% CATHOLIC**, and **62** or **%NO RELIG**.

	49) %FEM.WRK90	64) % BAPTIST	63) % CATHOLIC	62) %NO RELIG
49) %FEM.WRK90				
64) % BAPTIST				
63) % CATHOLIC				
62) %NO RELIG				

What is the correlation between **%FEM.WRK90** and **% BAPTIST**?   _____

Is the correlation statistically significant? (circle one)   Yes   No

What is the correlation between **%FEM.WRK90** and **% CATHOLIC**?   _____

Is the correlation statistically significant? (circle one)   Yes   No

What is the correlation between **%FEM.WRK90** and **%NO RELIG**?   _____

Is the correlation statistically significant? (circle one)   Yes   No

How would you describe the relationship between the female employment rate and religion? Why might this be?

6. *Press <ENTER>* to clear the screen for a new list of variables. This time, you can select your own dependent variable. When you are asked for the first variable, *type* **49) %FEM.WRK90**. Then select a variable that you think will be positively or negatively related to the female employment rate. (**Reminder:** You can use **F3** to see a list of the variables, or you can consult the list of variables in the back of your book and type in the name or number of the variable you wish to select.)

Which variable did you select?   _____

Write a hypothesis using **49) %FEM.WRK90** as the independent variable and the variable you selected as the dependent variable:

_____

_____

What is the correlation coefficient?   r = _____

Is the correlation statistically significant? (circle one)   Yes   No

Is the hypothesis supported or rejected? (circle one)   Supported   Rejected

Press **P** (for Print). (**Note:** If your computer is not connected to a printer, or if you have been instructed not to use the printer, skip these printing instructions. Instead, draw a table on a separate sheet of paper showing the final results.) Attach a copy of your results.

Explain why you think your hypothesis was, or was not, supported.

◆ CHAPTER 9 ◆
Marital Happiness

Most people go into marriage with the expectation that their relationships with their spouses will be sources of personal happiness and fulfillment. Although people may believe that economic and social concerns are important, in modern societies, emotional fulfillment is usually the most important benchmark used to judge the quality of a marital relationship. People want more than just a stable relationship—they want to be *happily* married. But not every marriage can be described as happy. Even marriages that last a lifetime vary with regard to how much personal fulfillment each partner derives from the relationship. In this chapter, we will attempt to explain some of the variation in marital happiness and look for connections between marital happiness and other social characteristics.

Open the **NORC** data file and go to the **Univariate Statistics** function on the **STATISTICAL ANALYSIS MENU**. Select **59** or **HAPPY.MAR?** as your variable. *Press <ENTER> to skip the* subset option. You will see this pie chart on your screen:

IF CURRENTLY MARRIED: Taking things all together, how would you describe your marriage? Would you say that your marriage is very happy, pretty happy, or not too happy?

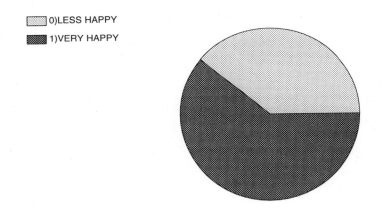

☐ 0)LESS HAPPY
■ 1)VERY HAPPY

The survey question as it was originally worded is shown across the top of your screen. The respondents were asked to describe their marriage using three possible responses: "very happy," "pretty happy," or "not too happy." However, when you look at the pie chart, you see only two groups, and they are labeled "very happy" and "less happy." The reason for the discrepancy is that only 6 percent of the respondents indicated that their marriage was "not too happy." Such a small percentage makes it difficult to use with tabular statistics. Therefore, the categories "not too happy" and "pretty happy" were combined and labeled "less happy." Looking at the chart, we see that even when these two categories are combined, the majority of respondents describe their marriages as "very happy."

Are marriages in our society really that happy? Perhaps—but researchers have found that even people who are not happily married may be reluctant to say so in an interview with a social researcher. Why? Some people may not be forthcoming because they are concerned with the way they appear to others—happy marriages are seen as an indicator of social and personal stability.

Others may not even want to admit their interpersonal failures to themselves. By the time some people get around to acknowledging the poor quality of their marriage relationships, they will have already separated or divorced—in which case they will be dropped from this subsample altogether. Thus, it is very difficult to locate those who identify themselves as unhappily married. As you complete this exercise, you should keep in mind the limitations of the variables we used to measure the quality of marital relationships.

Even using this rough measure of marital happiness, we can observe some interesting differences. For example, go to the **Tabular Statistics** function and select **59** or **HAPPY.MAR?** as your row variable and **13** or **# CHILDREN** as your column variable. *Press <ENTER>* twice to skip the control and subset variable options. After the table appears on your screen, *press* **C** (for Column percentages). Here are the percentaged results:

	NONE	1–2	3 OR MORE
LESS HAPPY	26.0	39.7	43.1
VERY HAPPY	74.0	60.3	56.9

The pattern is quite clear: the more children a couple has, the less likely they are to describe their relationship as very happy. Those with no children are the most likely to say they are very happily married (74 percent), and those with three or more children are the least likely to describe their marriage as very happy (56.9 percent). *Type* **S** (for Statistics) and you will see that the results are statistically significant (Prob. = 0.000). The raising of children requires time and energy, which means that there is less of both of these resources to devote to the marriage relationship.

Because women are more likely than men to spend much of their day with their children, we can hypothesize that **children will have more of an impact on marital happiness for women than for men.** To test this hypothesis, again select **59** or **HAPPY.MAR?** as your row variable and **13** or **# CHILDREN** as your column variable, but this time, use **1** or **SEX** as the control variable. *Press <ENTER>* several times until the first table appears. *Press* **C** (for Column percentages). These results for males will be shown first as indicated at the top left corner of the screen:

MALES

	NONE	1–2	3 OR MORE
LESS HAPPY	31.6	37.5	40.0
VERY HAPPY	68.4	62.5	60.0

The results appear to be similar to those in the preceding table, but *type* **S** (for Statistics) and you will see that the differences are not statistically significant (Prob. = 0.1666). *Press <ENTER>* once to return to the table showing the results for MALES, then *press <ENTER>* again to see the table for FEMALES. The label "FEMALE" should appear at the top left corner of the screen. *Type* **C** (for Column percentages). The following results for females appear on your screen:

FEMALES

	NONE	1–2	3 OR MORE
LESS HAPPY	20.2	41.5	46.1
VERY HAPPY	79.8	58.5	53.9

Press **S** (for Statistics). The difference is statistically significant (Prob. = 0.000); therefore, the hypothesis is supported. Even when using this crude measure of marital happiness, we can see that the presence of children in the home does not affect men and women equally. Children detract from marital satisfaction for women, but have no effect on marital satisfaction for men.

Now it's your turn. In the exercises that follow, you will have the opportunity to see how marital happiness is related to some other social, economic, and familial factors.

WORKSHEET

NAME:

COURSE:

DATE:

EXERCISE
9

Open the **NORC** data file and select the **Tabular Statistics** function.

1. Because those who have been divorced will have learned from their previous marriages what they desire in a mate, **those who have previously been divorced will be more likely to say they are very happy with their current marriages.**

   Make **59** or **HAPPY.MAR?** the row variable and **7** or **EVER DIVOR** the column variable. When the final table appears, *press* **C** (for Column percentages). Fill in the table below.

	YES	NO
LESS HAPPY	%	%
VERY HAPPY	%	%

Prob. = _____

V = _____

Is the difference statistically significant? (circle one)   Yes   No

Is the hypothesis supported or rejected? (circle one)   Supported   Rejected

Were these the results you expected? Explain.

2. Make **59** or **HAPPY.MAR?** the row variable and **30** or **CLASS** the column variable. Remember to *press* **C** (for Column percentages). Fill in the table.

	LOWER	WORKING	MIDDLE	UPPER
LESS HAPPY	%	%	%	%
VERY HAPPY	%	%	%	%

Prob. = _____

V = _____

Is the difference statistically significant? (circle one)   Yes   No

Use **F3** to examine the complete variable description for **37) CHANGE $?**. As you can see, this is another indicator of family finances. Use **59** or **HAPPY.MAR?** as the row variable and use **37** or **CHANGE $?** as the column variable. Use column percentaging for the final table. Fill in the results.

	BETTER	WORSE	THE SAME
LESS HAPPY	%	%	%
VERY HAPPY	%	%	%

Prob. = _____

V = _____

Is the difference statistically significant? (circle one)   Yes   No

Carefully read the percentaged results of this table. Now, summarize the relationship between family income and marital satisfaction based on the last two tables.

3. Again use **F3** to examine the complete variable description for **38) LIKE JOB?**. Now, make **59** or **HAPPY.MAR?** the row variable and **38** or **LIKE JOB?** the column variable. Remember to percentage your table properly. Fill in the results below.

	VERY SAT.	MODER.SAT.	DISSATIS
LESS HAPPY	%	%	%
VERY HAPPY	%	%	%

Prob. = _____

V = _____

Is the difference statistically significant? (circle one)   Yes   No

Summarize the results of this table in one or two sentences. Then explain why you believe these results occurred.

4. Because television can keep couples from conversing or engaging in other social activities, **couples who spend more time watching television will be less happy with their marriages.**

Make **59** or **HAPPY.MAR?** the row variable and **93** or **WATCH TV** the column variable. Make sure to properly percentage the final results. Fill in the table.

	0–1 HOUR	1–2 HOURS	2–3 HOURS
LESS HAPPY	%	%	%
VERY HAPPY	%	%	%

Prob. = _____

V = _____

Is the difference statistically significant? (circle one)   Yes   No

Is the hypothesis supported or rejected? (circle one)   Supported   Rejected

Were these the results you expected? Explain.

5. Because camping requires cooperation and gives families time to be together, **couples who go camping together will be more likely to say they are very happy with their marriages.**

    Make **59** or **HAPPY.MAR?** the row variable and **94** or **CAMPING** the column variable. Percentage the results and fill in the table.

	YES	NO
LESS HAPPY	%	%
VERY HAPPY	%	%

Prob. = _____

V = _____

Is the difference statistically significant? (circle one)   Yes   No

Is the hypothesis supported or rejected? (circle one)   Supported   Rejected

What might be a reason the hypothesis was, or was not, supported?

6. Make **59** or **HAPPY.MAR?** the row variable and **50** or **HOW RELIG?** the column variable. Percentage the results and fill in the table.

	STRONG	SOMEWHAT	NOT VERY
LESS HAPPY	%	%	%
VERY HAPPY	%	%	%

Prob. = _____

V = _____

Is the difference statistically significant? (circle one)   Yes   No

How would you explain these results?

7. Now it's time to test your own hypothesis. Remember, you can use **F3** to view and select variables, or you can consult the list of variables in the back of your book and type in the name or number of the variable you wish to select.

    Write a hypothesis using **59** or **HAPPY.MAR?** as either the independent (cause) or dependent (effect) variable:

    _____

    _____

    What is your dependent variable?   _____
    (make this your row variable)

    What is your independent variable?   _____
    (make this your column variable)

    Type **C** (for Column percentages). *Press* **P** (for Print). (**Note:** If your computer is not connected to a printer, or you have been instructed not to use the printer, skip these instructions. Instead, draw a table on a separate sheet of paper showing the final, percentaged results.) Attach a copy of the results.

    Is the difference statistically significant? (circle one)   Yes   No

    Is the hypothesis supported or rejected? (circle one)   Supported   Rejected

    Discuss why you think your hypothesis was or was not supported.

◆ CHAPTER 10 ◆
Marital and Extramarital Sex

Sexual intercourse is an aspect of married life that most people value—but are often reluctant to talk about. As a result, there is some uncertainty as to what is *typical* with regard to a married couple's sex life. For example, how often do most couples have sexual intercourse? How does the presence of children in the household affect a couple's sex life? How common are extramarital affairs? These are a few of the questions we will try to address in this exercise.

Open the **NORC** data file and go to the **Univariate Statistics** function. When you are asked for the name or number of the variable you wish to examine, *type* **60** or **FREQ.SEX** and *press <ENTER>*. When you are prompted for the name or number of the subset variable, *type* **4** or **MARITAL** and *press <ENTER>*. We want to limit this analysis to persons who are currently married, so *type* **1** for the minimum value and *press <ENTER>*. *Type* **1** again for the maximum value and *press <ENTER>*. This figure will appear:

About how often did you have sex in the last 12 months?

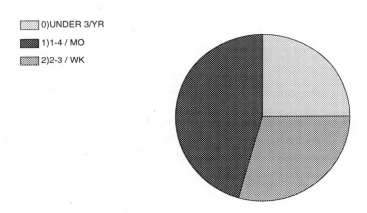

- ▨ 0)UNDER 3/YR
- ■ 1)1-4 / MO
- ▦ 2)2-3 / WK

Press **T** (for Table) to look at the distribution.

	FREQUENCY	%
UNDER 3/YR	532	25.1
1–4/MO	963	45.4
2–3/WK	624	29.4

As one might expect, there is a great deal of variation in the frequency of sexual intercourse among married couples. Nearly half (45.4 percent) fall into the middle range of 1 to 4 times per month; the rest are fairly evenly divided between under three times per year (25.1 percent) and 2 to 3 times per week (29.4 percent). The UNDER 3/YR category includes those married couples who did not have any sexual intercourse in the last 12 months. Let's see if we can uncover some of the factors that predict how sexually active a married couple is likely to be.

Press <ENTER> twice to return to the **STATISTICAL ANALYSIS MENU**. Move the highlight to **B. Tabular Statistics** and *press <ENTER>*. When you are asked for the name or number of the row variable, *type* **60** or **FREQ.SEX** and *press* *<ENTER>*. When you are asked for the name or number of the column variable, *type* **59** or **HAPPY.MAR?** and *press* *<ENTER>*. *Press* *<ENTER>* twice to skip the control variable and subset options. When the table appears, *press* **C** (for Column percentages).

	LESS HAPPY	VERY HAPPY
UNDER 3/YR	33.0	20.2
1–4/MO	42.3	47.4
2–3/WK	24.7	32.5

It appears that there is a relationship between marital happiness and the frequency of sexual intercourse. Among the very happily married, 32.5 percent have sexual intercourse 2 to 3 times per week, as compared to 24.7 percent for those who are less happily married. On the other hand, one third of those who are less happily married have sexual intercourse under three times a year. *Press* **S** (for Statistics). Prob. = 0.000, which means that the difference is statistically significant. Although our hypothesis is supported, we cannot be certain which is the cause and which is the effect. Do couples have intercourse more frequently because they are happy with their relationship? Or are couples happy with their relationship because they engage in sexual intercourse more often? Most likely it is a reciprocal relationship, in which each variable has a positive effect on the other.

For health-related reasons, one would think that **older couples will be less likely to have sexual intercourse 2 to 3 times per week.** *Press* *<ENTER>* twice to get ready for a new table. Use **60** or **FREQ.SEX** as the row variable and **2** or **AGE** as the column variable. *Press* *<ENTER>* once to skip the control variable option. When you are asked for the name or number of the variable to be used for subset 1, *type* **4** or **MARITAL** and *press* *<ENTER>*. *Type* **1** for the minimum value and *press* *<ENTER>*. *Type* **1** for the maximum value and *press* *<ENTER>* twice. When the table appears, *press* **C** (for Column percentages). This screen will appear:

	18–29	30–39	40–49	50–64	65 & OVER
UNDER 3/YR	3.5	12.6	18.4	31.7	69.4
1–4/MO	40.2	46.5	54.7	50.6	25.5
2–3/WK	56.4	40.9	26.9	17.7	5.2

The direction of the results is clearly consistent with the hypothesis. The 18- to 29-year-olds are the most likely to have sexual intercourse 2 to 3 times per week (56.4 percent). The next most sexually active group is the 30- to 39-year-olds, 40.9 percent of whom have sexual intercourse twice per week or more. Among those who are 65 or older, only 5.2 percent have sexual intercourse twice per week or more, while 69.4 have sex less than three times per year. *Press* **S** to look at the statistics. Prob. = 0.000. The hypothesis is supported.

Another factor that may influence the frequency of sexual intercourse is the presence of children. Children in the home can limit privacy and opportunities for spontaneity, and also drain emotional reserves and romantic energy. Thus, the hypothesis is: **The more children a couple has, the less likely they are to have sex 2 to 3 times per week.** Use **60** or **FREQ.SEX** as the row variable and **13** or **# CHILDREN** as the column variable. The subset variable is again **4** or **MARITAL**, with a minimum value of **1** and a maximum value of **1**. Use column percentaging for the final table.

	NONE	1–2	3 OR MORE
UNDER 3/YR	18.2	22.5	31.9
1–4/MO	44.8	46.5	44.1
2–3/WK	37.0	31.0	24.0

The most sexually active couples are those without children, 37 percent of whom have intercourse at least twice per week. In contrast, only 24 percent of those with three or more children have intercourse that often. *Type* **S** (for Statistics). The difference is statistically significant. The results are consistent with the hypothesis: more children means less sexual intercourse.

Let's look at one more factor that may influence the frequency of sexual intercourse for married couples: religion. Conservative religious groups have traditionally had very clear proscriptions against premarital sex. Does this have a lingering effect on the marriage? The hypothesis is: **Couples who attend fundamentalist churches will be less likely to have sex 2 to 3 times per week.** Select **60** or **FREQ.SEX** as the row variable and **52** or **R.FUND/LIB** as the column variable. The subset variable is **4** or **MARITAL** with a minimum value of **1** and a maximum value of **1**. When the final table appears, *press* **C** (for Column percentages). This is what your results will look like:

	FUNDAMENT.	MODERATE	LIBERAL
UNDER 3/YR	24.6	20.5	27.1
1–4/MO	43.6	46.5	45.5
2–3/WK	31.9	28.5	27.4

Contrary to the hypothesis, there are only slight differences among religious fundamentalists (31.9 percent), moderates (28.5 percent), and liberals (27.4 percent). So this hypothesis is rejected.

Thus far, we have looked at the frequency of sexual intercourse between marital partners. In the exercises that follow, you will be able to examine the nature and frequency of extramarital sexual intercourse.

Your turn.

WORKSHEET

NAME:

COURSE:

DATE:

EXERCISE
10

Open the **NORC** data file and select the **Univariate Statistics** function.

1. Obtain a pie chart for **67** or **XMAR.SEX**. *Press* **T** (for Table) and fill in the results below:

	FREQUENCY	%
ALWAYS WRG		
ALMOST AL.		
SOMETIMES		
NOT AT ALL		

Now select variable **61** or **EVER STRAY**. Examine the wording of the question and fill in the results below.

	FREQUENCY	%
YES		
NO		

Return to the **STATISTICAL ANALYSIS MENU** and select **B. Tabular Statistics**. For the row variable select **61** or **EVER STRAY**. For the column variable select **67** or **XMAR.SEX**. *Press <ENTER>* twice to skip the control variable and subset options. *Press* **C** (for Column percentages). Fill in the table.

	ALWAYS WRG	ALMOST AL.	SOMETIMES	NOT AT ALL
YES	%	%	%	%
NO	%	%	%	%

Prob. = _____

V = _____

Is the difference statistically significant? (circle one)   Yes   No

Overall, how would you describe people's attitudes toward extramarital sex and their behavior?

2. Go back to **Univariate Statistics**. Select **62** or **FRIEND SEX** as the variable you wish to examine. When you are asked for the name or number of the subset variable, *type* **4** or **MARI-TAL** and *press <ENTER>*. *Type* **1** for the minimum value and *press <ENTER>*. *Type* **1** for the maximum value and *press <ENTER>*. This limits the analysis to those who are currently married. When the pie chart appears on the screen be sure to read the question wording. Then *press* **T** (for Table) and fill in the results below.

	FREQUENCY	%
YES		
NO		

Press <ENTER> to get ready to examine a new variable. This time, select **63** or **PICKUP SEX**. Again, use **4** or **MARITAL** as the subset variable, with a minimum value of **1** and a maximum value of **1**. Read the question wording, then *press* **T** (for Table) and fill in the results below.

	FREQUENCY	%
YES		
NO		

Press <ENTER>. Select **64** or **PAID SEX?** as the variable you wish to examine. Again use **4** or **MARITAL** as the subset variable, with a minimum value of **1** and a maximum value of **1**. *Press* **T** (for Table) and fill in the results below.

	FREQUENCY	%
YES		
NO		

Briefly summarize the results of these analyses. Then discuss what these results suggest to you about the nature of extramarital sexual activity.

3. The hypothesis is: **Men will be more likely than women to have ever had an extramarital affair.**

    Select **Tabular Statistics** and make **61** or **EVER STRAY** the row variable and **1** or **SEX** the column variable. *Press <ENTER>* twice to skip the control variable and subset option. *Press* **C** (for Column percentages) and fill in the table.

	MALE	FEMALE
YES	%	%
NO	%	%

    Prob. = _____

    V = _____

    Is the difference statistically significant? (circle one)   Yes   No

    Is the hypothesis supported or rejected? (circle one)   Supported   Rejected

    Were these the results you expected? Explain.

4. Because older people have been married longer, the hypothesis is: **The older people are, the more likely they are to have ever had an extramarital affair.**

    Make **61** or **EVER STRAY** the row variable and **2** or **AGE** the column variable. *Press* **C** (for Column percentages). Fill in the table.

	18–29	30–39	40–49	50–64	65 & OVER
YES	%	%	%	%	%
NO	%	%	%	%	%

Prob. = _____

V = _____

Is the difference statistically significant? (circle one)   Yes   No

Is the hypothesis supported or rejected? (circle one)   Supported   Rejected

How would you explain these results for those under age 65?

How would you explain these results for those over age 65?

5. The hypothesis is: **Religious fundamentalists will be less likely than moderates or liberals to have ever had an extramarital affair.**

   Make **61** or **EVER STRAY** the row variable and **52** or **R.FUND/LIB** the column variable. *Press* **C** (for Column percentages). Fill in the table.

	FUNDAMENT.	MODERATE	LIBERAL
YES	%	%	%
NO	%	%	%

Prob. = _____

V = _____

Is the difference statistically significant? (circle one)   Yes   No

Is the hypothesis supported or rejected? (circle one)   Supported   Rejected

The hypothesis is: **Those who attend church regularly will be less likely to have ever had an extramarital affair.**

Make **61** or **EVER STRAY** the row variable and **49** or **CH.ATTEND** the column variable. *Press* **C** (for Column percentages). Fill in the table.

	LESS OFTEN	ANNUALLY	MONTHLY	WEEKLY
YES	%	%	%	%
NO	%	%	%	%

Prob. = _____

V = _____

Is the difference statistically significant? (circle one)   Yes   No

Is the hypothesis supported or rejected? (circle one)   Supported   Rejected

Based on the above hypotheses, what would you conclude about the relationship between religion and extramarital sexual activity?

6. The hypothesis is: **Married women who are employed will be more likely to have had an extramarital affair.**

    Make **61** or **EVER STRAY** the row variable and **33** or **MAR.F.WRK** the column variable. *Press* **C** (for Column percentages). Fill in the table.

	FULL TIME	PART TIME	HOMEMAKER
YES	%	%	%
NO	%	%	%

Prob. = _____

V = _____

Is the difference statistically significant? (circle one) Yes No

Is the hypothesis supported or rejected? (circle one) Supported Rejected

Were these the results you expected? Explain.

7. The hypothesis is: **The more children people have, the less likely they are to have ever had an extramarital affair.**

Make **61** or **EVER STRAY** the row variable, **13** or **# CHILDREN** the column variable, and **1** or **SEX** the control variable. When the first table (MALES) appears, *press* **C** (for Column percentages). Fill in the tables.

MALES

	NONE	1–2	3 OR MORE
YES	%	%	%
NO	%	%	%

Prob. = _____

V = _____

Is the difference statistically significant? (circle one) Yes No

Is the hypothesis supported or rejected? (circle one) Supported Rejected

Press <ENTER> once to return to the table for MALES, and *press <ENTER>* again to see the table for FEMALES. Make sure to percentage the table properly, and then fill in the results below.

FEMALES

	NONE	1–2	3 OR MORE
YES	%	%	%
NO	%	%	%

Prob. = _____

V = _____

Is the difference statistically significant? (circle one)   Yes   No

Is the hypothesis supported or rejected? (circle one)   Supported   Rejected

Summarize any differences between the results for men and those for women. How would you explain these differences?

8. Now it's time to test your own hypothesis. Remember, you can use **F3** to view and select variables, or you can consult the list of variables in the back of your book and type in the name or number of the variable you wish to select.

Write a hypothesis using **61** or **EVER STRAY** as either the independent (cause) or dependent (effect) variable:

_____

_____

What is your dependent variable?
(make this your row variable)   _____

What is your independent variable?
(make this your column variable)   _____

Type **C** (for Column percentages). *Press* **P** (for Print). (**Note:** If your computer is not connected to a printer, or you have been instructed not to use the printer, skip these printing instructions. Instead, draw a table on a separate sheet of paper showing the final, percentaged results.) Attach a copy of the results.

Is the difference statistically significant? (circle one)   Yes   No

Is the hypothesis supported or rejected? (circle one)   Supported   Rejected

Discuss why you think your hypothesis was, or was not, supported.

CHAPTER 11

Fertility and Family Life

Among the most important decisions a couple must make is whether or not to have children. If a couple decides to have children, then the next question is how many. Their hope for a certain family size may or may not be realized. Some couples end up with more children than they had planned, others with fewer. In either case, the impact of children on the marriage relationship is still an important topic to explore. In this exercise, we will explore some variations in family size, then examine the impact of children on family life.

Open the **NORC** data file and go to the **Univariate Statistics** function. Select variable **13** or **# CHILDREN**. *Press <ENTER>* to skip the subset option.

How many children have you ever had? Please count all that were born alive at any time (including any you had from a previous marriage).

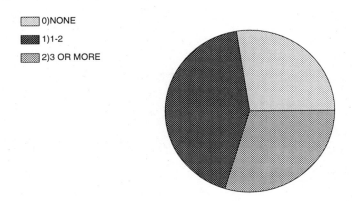

0)NONE
1)1-2
2)3 OR MORE

As you can see from the survey question, this figure illustrates how many children respondents have had over their lifetime. Nearly half of those surveyed have one or two children. The rest are fairly evenly divided between those who have three or more children and those who have none.

Most of us are aware that families today are having fewer children, so let's put the above distribution into historical perspective. One way we can do this is by dividing the sample into age "cohorts" and then comparing the younger generations with the older generations. *Press <ENTER>* twice to return to the **STATISTICAL ANALYSIS MENU**. Select **B. Tabular Statistics**. When you are asked for the name or number of the row variable, *type* **13** or **# CHILDREN** and *press <ENTER>*. When you are prompted for the name or number of the column variable, *type* **2** or **AGE** and *press <ENTER>*. *Press <ENTER>* twice. *Press* **C** (for Column percentages). These results will appear on your screen:

	18–29	30–39	40–49	50–64	65 & OVER
NONE	61.7	29.8	21.2	10.9	14.5
1–2	31.8	50.4	52.4	36.8	37.7
3 OR MORE	6.4	19.8	26.4	52.2	47.8

As you might expect, the older groups tend to have more children. The most distinct dividing line is at age 50. Look at the row labeled "3 or MORE." The percentage of respondents over age 50 with three or more children is more than double that of previous generations. Of course, these figures may be deceiving, because many of the younger respondents are likely to have more children in the future. However, a reversal of the trend toward smaller families seems unlikely.

Why are Americans choosing to have fewer children? Part of the answer may be related to the increase in the number of dual-earner families. When both parents are employed, there is less time available to devote to parenting, especially if both parents are employed full-time (dual-career families). Thus, two-income families are likely to have fewer children so that they can balance their work and family roles. Families in which one spouse is a full-time homemaker, on the other hand, will probably have more children, because there is more time to devote to parenting and because more of the homemaker's identity is derived from the parenting role. Dual-earner families, in which both spouses are employed but at least one works only part-time, will fall in the middle. Therefore, the hypothesis is: **Married couples with only one employed spouse will have the most children and couples in which both spouses have careers will have the fewest children.** *Press <ENTER>* to clear the screen for a new table. This time, use **13** or **# CHILDREN** as your row variable and **34** or **FAM.WORK** as your column variable. Skip the control and subset options. *Press* **C** (for Column percentages). Here is what your results will look like:

	1 FULLTIME	FULL&PART	2 FULLTIME
NONE	7.8	11.7	21.0
1–2	53.3	55.6	55.7
3 OR MORE	38.9	32.7	23.3

The results are consistent with our hypothesis. Looking first at couples with no children, we see that dual-career families (7.8 percent) are more likely than dual-earner couples who have at least one spouse working part-time (11.7 percent) or single-earner families (21 percent) to fall into this category. On the other hand, 38.9 percent of single-earner families have three or more children, as compared to 32.7 percent for dual-earner families and 23.3 percent for dual-career families. *Press* **S** (for Statistics). The difference is statistically significant (Prob. = 0.000). The hypothesis is supported. In industrialized societies, where work usually takes place outside the home, married couples have reduced their family size to make parenting more manageable.

In addition to affecting the dynamics of everyday family life, industrialization creates a demand for an educated work force. Today, most people receive at least some college training. For many young people, going to college will delay marriage and/or childbearing. The investment in a college degree may also lead to a greater commitment to the workplace after graduation—which, as we have already seen, limits family size. Either way, we would hypothesize that **those who have more education will have fewer children.** *Press <ENTER>* twice to clear the screen for a new table. Use **13** or **# CHILDREN** as the row variable and **42** or **DEGREE** as the column variable. Skip the control and subset options. *Type* **C** (for Column percentages). Here are your results:

	NOT H.S.	HIGH SCH.	JR. COL.	B.A.	GRAD. DEG.
NONE	21.2	25.3	27.1	38.4	34.7
1–2	35.2	45.1	50.2	40.7	42.2
3 OR MORE	43.6	29.6	22.7	20.9	23.1

Our hypothesis appears to be supported: the percentage of respondents having three or more children decreases as the education level increases. The most notable difference is among those who did not finish high school. Over 40 percent of those who do not have a high school degree have three or more children. Of course, it is hard to say which comes first. Did having children lead to dropping out of school, or did dropping out of school lead to having more children? We can get a partial answer to this question by seeing whether those with less education have a desire for larger families. *Press <ENTER>* once to clear the screen for a new table. This time, use **15** or **IDEAL#KIDS** as the row variable and **42** or **DEGREE** as the column variable. After you *press* **C** (for Column percentages), this screen will appear:

	NOT H.S.	HIGH SCH.	JR. COL.	B.A.	GRAD. DEG.
TWO OR LESS	56.1	65.3	67.8	62.7	66.7
THREE OR M	43.9	34.7	32.2	37.3	33.3

Although there is an overall preference for smaller families, even among those who completed high school, respondents who did not complete high school are more likely to want three or more children (43.9 percent). *Type* **S** (for Statistics) and you will see that the difference is statistically significant (Prob. = 0.000). We can conclude from these results that the tendency for those who are less educated to have larger families cannot be reduced to a mere lack of knowledge of contraceptives, resulting in unwanted pregnancies. It may be that those who drop out of the education system, and consequently lack access to many economic opportunities, seek to find their identity elsewhere—for example, in their families.

Let's look for some other cultural variations. Select **13** or **# CHILDREN** for the row variable and **3** or **WH/BLACK** for the column variable. Use column percentaging for the table. Your results will look like this:

	WHITE	BLACK
NONE	28.5	20.3
1–2	43.0	40.4
3 OR MORE	28.5	39.3

Whites are more likely than African Americans to have no children, and African Americans are more likely than whites to have three or more children. *Press* **S** (for Statistics) and you will see that the difference is statistically significant (Prob. = 0.000). Are these differences based on a difference in cultural values—or do they result from fewer educational and economic opportunities? We can partially answer this question by controlling for education. Again, use **13** or **# CHILDREN** for the row variable and **3** or **WH/BLACK** for the column variable. *Press <ENTER>* once to skip the control variable option. This time, when you are asked for a subset variable, select **42** or **DEGREE**, with a minimum value of **2** (junior college) and a maximum value of **4** (graduate school). When the final results appear, *press* **C** (for Column percentages):

	WHITE	BLACK
NONE	36.1	24.0
1–2	41.6	56.3
3 OR MORE	22.3	19.8

When we look only at the subset of those who have at least some college education, the results are quite different. Whites continue to be more likely to have no children, but they are also the most likely to have three or more children. African Americans are more concentrated in the middle, with one or two children. Thus, we can conclude that the tendency for African Americans to have larger families than whites overall is more a result of educational opportunities than of cultural differences.

Finally, let's look at another cultural variable that many assume to be related to family size—religion. Because the Catholic church officially forbids the use of contraceptives, we would hypothesize that **Catholics will be the most likely to have three or more children**. To test this hypothesis, select **13** or **# CHILDREN** as your row variable and **51** or **RELIGION** as your column variable. Do not select a control or subset variable. *Press* **C** (for Column percentages). These results will appear:

	PROTESTANT	CATHOLIC	JEWISH	NONE
NONE	23.3	30.3	39.1	43.1
1–2	45.1	38.2	48.9	38.1
3 OR MORE	31.7	31.5	12.0	18.8

The results do not support the hypothesis. Virtually the same percentage of Protestants and Catholics have three or more children. There is a difference, however, when one compares these two categories with the remaining ones. Protestants and Catholics are far more likely than all other religious categories, including respondents with no religious affiliation, to have three or more children.

Let's take a closer look at the Protestants to see whether all Protestants are the same in regard to number of children. Because fundamentalists are generally less supportive of women's working outside the home, we could hypothesize that **religious fundamentalists will be more likely than religious liberals to have three or more children**. Again, use **13** or **# CHILDREN** as your row variable, only this time use **52** or **R.FUND/LIB** as the column variable. *Press <ENTER>* to skip the control and subset options. *Press* **C** (for Column percentages) and look at your results:

	FUNDAMENT.	MODERATE	LIBERAL
NONE	22.0	28.7	31.4
1–2	43.7	40.8	44.5
3 OR MORE	34.3	30.5	24.1

The hypothesis is supported. Religious fundamentalists are more likely than either moderates or liberals to have three or more children, and the difference is statistically significant (Prob. = 0.000).

So far, we have looked at reasons why families may vary in size—but why is this important? What effect do children have on their parents? In the exercises, you will have the opportunity to explore these questions on your own.

Your turn.

WORKSHEET

NAME:

COURSE:

DATE:

If you have not already done so, open the **NORC** data file.

1. Go to the **Univariate Statistics** function and select variable **20) KIDS JOY**. *Type* **D** (for Distribution). Read the survey question at the top of the screen and then fill in the table.

	FREQUENCY	%
STRG.AGREE		
AGREE		
NEITHER		
DISAGREE		
STRG.DISAG		

Press <ENTER> three times to return to the **STATISTICAL ANALYSIS MENU** and select **B. Tabular Statistics**. Make **58** or **HAPPY?** the row variable and **13** or **# CHILDREN** the column variable. When you are asked for a control variable, select **1** or **SEX**. When the first table (MALES) appears, *press* **C** (for Column percentages). Fill in the table.

MALES

	NONE	1–2	3 OR MORE
VERY HAPPY	%	%	%
PRET.HAPPY	%	%	%
NOT TOO	%	%	%

Prob. = _____

V = _____

Is the difference statistically significant? (circle one)   Yes   No

Press *<ENTER>* once to return to the table for MALES, and *press <ENTER>* again to see the table for females. *Press* **C** (for Column percentages).

FEMALES

	NONE	1–2	3 OR MORE
VERY HAPPY	%	%	%
PRET.HAPPY	%	%	%
NOT TOO	%	%	%

Prob. = _____

V = _____

Is the difference statistically significant? (circle one)   Yes   No

How would you summarize the relationship between children and personal happiness?

2. Return to the **STATISTICAL ANALYSIS MENU** and select **A. Univariate Statistics**. Select **19** or **KID.NOFREE** and *press <ENTER>* twice. Read the wording at the top of the screen. Now, *type* **D** (for Distribution) and fill in the table below.

	FREQUENCY	%
STRG.AGREE		
AGREE		
NEITHER		
DISAGREE		
STRG.DISAG		

How would you answer this survey question? Do you think your current lifestyle and activities will be affected if or when you have children? (If you already have children, do you think they interfere with your freedom?) Explain your answer.

3. The remaining questions examine the impact children actually have on certain activities. Before conducting the analysis for each table, use **F3** to examine the complete variable descriptions of the variables being used. Switch to the **Tabular Statistics** option and make **87** or **GO SPORT** the row variable and **13** or **# CHILDREN** the column variable. Remember to percentage the table and fill in the results.

	NONE	1–2	3 OR MORE
YES	%	%	%
NO	%	%	%

Prob. = _____

V = _____

Is the difference statistically significant? (circle one)   Yes   No

Create and fill in the table below. Make **88** or **GO MUSIC** the row variable and **13** or **# CHILDREN** the column variable. Remember to percentage the table and fill in the results.

	NONE	1–2	3 OR MORE
YES	%	%	%
NO	%	%	%

Prob. = _____

V = _____

Is the difference statistically significant? (circle one)   Yes   No

Do these last two results seem consistent with your answer for Question 2? Explain.

4. Create and fill in the table below. Make **89** or **CRAFTS** the row variable and **13** or **# CHILDREN** the column variable. Remember to percentage the table and fill in the results.

	NONE	1–2	3 OR MORE
YES	%	%	%
NO	%	%	%

Prob. = _____

V = _____

Is the difference statistically significant? (circle one)   Yes   No

Create and fill in the table below. Make **90** or **GARDEN** the row variable and **13** or **# CHILDREN** the column variable. Remember to percentage the table and fill in the results.

	NONE	1–2	3 OR MORE
YES	%	%	%
NO	%	%	%

Prob. = _____

V = _____

Is the difference statistically significant? (circle one)   Yes   No

Are these results consistent with your answer for Question 2? Explain.

5. Create and fill in the table below. Make **94** or **CAMPING** the row variable and **13** or **# CHILDREN** the column variable. Remember to percentage the table and fill in the results.

	NONE	1–2	3 OR MORE
YES	%	%	%
NO	%	%	%

Prob. = _____

V = _____

Is the difference statistically significant? (circle one)   Yes   No

Make **91** or **HUNT/FISH** the row variable and **13** or **# CHILDREN** the column variable. Fill in the percentaged results for the table.

	NONE	1–2	3 OR MORE
YES	%	%	%
NO	%	%	%

Prob. = _____

V = _____

Is the difference statistically significant? (circle one)   Yes   No

6. Make **92** or **SEE MOVIE** the row variable and **13** or **# CHILDREN** the column variable. Fill in the percentaged results for the table.

	NONE	1–2	3 OR MORE
YES	%	%	%
NO	%	%	%

Prob. = _____

V = _____

Is the difference statistically significant? (circle one)   Yes   No

Make **93** or **WATCH TV** the row variable and **13** or **# CHILDREN** the column variable. Fill in the percentaged results for the table.

	NONE	1–2	3 OR MORE
0–1 HOUR	%	%	%
1–2 HOURS	%	%	%
2–3 HOURS	%	%	%

Prob. = _____

V = _____

Is the difference statistically significant? (circle one)   Yes   No

Are these last two results consistent with your answer for Question 2? Explain.

7. Now it's time to test your own hypothesis. Remember, you can use **F3** to view and select variables, or you can consult the list of variables in the back of your book and type in the name or number of the variable you wish to select.

    Write a hypothesis using **13) # CHILDREN** or **15) IDEAL#KIDS** as either the independent (cause) or dependent (effect) variable.

    _____

    _____

    What is your dependent variable?   _____
    (make this your row variable)

    What is your independent variable?   _____
    (make this your column variable)

Type **C** (for Column percentages). *Press* **P** (for Print). (**Note:** If your computer is not connected to a printer, or you have been instructed not to use the printer, skip these printing instructions. Instead, draw a table on a separate sheet of paper showing the final, percentaged results.) Attach a copy of the results.

    Is the difference statistically significant? (circle one)   Yes   No

    Is the hypothesis supported or rejected? (circle one)   Supported   Rejected

Discuss why you think your hypothesis was, or was not, supported.

8. Based on all the results above, how would you summarize the effects children have on lifestyles?

Explain why some activities are affected more than others.

◆ CHAPTER 12 ◆
Childrearing

In 1956, Melvin L. Kohn conducted a study of the values guiding childrearing practices among American parents.[1] His findings indicated two very distinctive clusters of childrearing values and showed that parents of higher social status put more stress on one while lower-status parents put more stress on the other.

Lower-status parents tended to put greater emphasis on values such as good manners, obedience, neatness, and cleanliness than did higher-status parents. In contrast, higher-status parents placed greater value on curiosity, responsibility, and consideration for others (Kohn, 1959). Kohn identified the first value cluster as concern about *conforming* to norms, and the second as concern about *self-expression and self-direction*. Over the years Kohn, with various associates (especially Carmi Schooler), has restudied childrearing values and has had similar findings, even in other countries (Pearlin and Kohn, 1966; Kohn and Schooler, 1969, 1983). To explain these results, Kohn and his associates theorize as follows:

Parents try to give their children the best possible chances in life. To do so, they try to instill in them what they have learned from their life experiences about how the world works and how best to get along. Lower-status parents tend to hold the kinds of jobs in which they do well to the extent that they are regarded as dependable—as people who are prompt, who show up at work looking neat and clean, who have adequate manners, and who obey the rules. In contrast, higher-status parents have found that they are more successful in their jobs when they can take individual initiative, are responsible and curious, and have good interpersonal skills. So parents draw on their own experiences in deciding how to raise their children. To the extent that children grow up and take jobs similar to those held by their parents, such a pattern may be quite functional. On the other hand, it might cause people simply to end up in the same kinds of jobs as their parents because of the ways they were socialized.

Keep in mind that these patterns are simply tendencies; *all* parents probably value all of the qualities presented to them in Kohn's research. But as we take a look at some similar childrearing values from the GSS data set, we will expect to find the same patterns along social-status lines.

To begin, let's look at a measure that asks respondents to decide whether they think it is more important for parents to emphasize obedience or independent thinking. Kohn's theory would predict that **lower-status parents will believe parents should stress obedience, while upper-status parents will believe that parents should stress independent thinking.**

Open the **NORC** data file and go to the **STATISTICAL ANALYSIS MENU**. Place the highlight on **B. Tabular Statistics** and *press <ENTER>*. *Press* **F3** and examine the variable description for **21) KID OBEY**. When you are finished, close the codebook windows by *pressing <ENTER>* and select **21** or **KID OBEY** a*s* the row variable. When you are asked for the name or number of the column variable, *type* **30** or **CLASS** and *press <ENTER>*. *Press <ENTER>* twice to skip the control and subset options. When the table appears on the screen, *press* **C** (for Column percentages). These are the results you will see:

---

[1] Portions of this exercise are based on presentations written by Rodney Stark and published in *Family and Gender*, MicroCase Corporation, 1987.

	LOWER	WORKING	MIDDLE	UPPER
OBEDIENT	46.8	35.5	25.9	22.4
THINK	53.2	64.5	74.1	77.6

As you might expect, there is a clear difference along class lines. As social status increases, the emphasis placed on obedience declines. Parents from the upper class (22.4 percent) are less than half as likely as parents from the lower class (46.8 percent) to believe that parents should emphasize obedience more than independent thinking. Is the difference statistically significant? *Press* **S** (for Statistics). Prob. = 0.000, so the difference is statistically significant and the hypothesis is supported.

Because education is highly correlated with social class, and because colleges tend to emphasize independent thinking, we would expect similar results using education as the independent variable. *Press <ENTER>* twice to clear the screen for a new table. Again, use **21** or **KID OBEY** as the row variable, but this time use **42** or **DEGREE** as the column variable. Use column percentaging for the table. Here are the results:

	NOT H.S.	HIGH SCH.	JR. COL.	B.A.	GRAD. DEG.
OBEDIENT	51.4	33.5	23.8	16.1	9.5
THINK	48.6	66.5	76.2	83.9	90.5

The results here are even more pronounced than those in the previous table. Those who did not graduate from high school (51.4 percent) are over three times more likely than those who hold a bachelor's degree (16.1 percent) to believe that parents should stress obedience more than independent thinking. It would appear that educational experiences are at least as important as, if not more important than, work experiences in shaping our childrearing practices.

So far, we have seen consistent support for Kohn's theory, but let's look at some of the other childrearing values studied by Kohn. For example, Kohn believed that upper-status parents are more likely to emphasize consideration for others. Therefore, the hypothesis is: **Parents from the upper class will be more likely to believe that parents should emphasize the importance of helping others.** Select **22** or **HELP OTHRS** as the row variable and **30** or **CLASS** as the column variable. Use column percentaging for the table. These are the results:

	LOWER	WORKING	MIDDLE	UPPER
MOST IMPOR	24.0	12.2	12.2	11.8
LESS IMPOR	76.0	87.8	87.8	88.2

The results are the opposite of those predicted by the hypothesis. Those who identify themselves as being from the lower class (24 percent) are more than twice as likely as those who say they are from the upper class (11.8 percent) to say that helping others is the most important value parents should teach their children. If you look at the statistics, you will see that the difference is statistically significant (Prob. = 0.000). It could be that those who have the fewest financial resources are more aware of the need for people to help each other during times of need. Financial security may lead people to believe that everyone should be self-sufficient and not dependent on help from others.

Along with the idea of self-sufficiency, we might expect that **upper-status parents will be more likely to emphasize the value of hard work** as a means of maintaining independence. Make **23** or **WORK HARD** the row variable and **30** or **CLASS** the column variable. *Press* **C** (for Column percentages). Here are the results:

	LOWER	WORKING	MIDDLE	UPPER
MOST IMPOR	12.9	14.1	15.1	15.5
LESS IMPOR	87.1	85.9	84.9	84.5

The differences here are not as great as those we have seen previously. *Press* **S** (for Statistics). In fact, Prob. = 0.799, so the differences we do see are not statistically significant. Social class does not have a significant impact on the emphasis parents place on the value of hard work.

Social status is not the only factor that influences childrearing values. We would expect other cultural distinctions, such as race or religion, to be important as well. Let's start by taking a look at race. Does people's race have any bearing on the values they stress with their children? Make **21** or **KID OBEY** the row variable and **3** or **WH/BLACK** the column variable. Because we know that social status is related both to race and to childrearing values, we should control for social class. *Press* <*ENTER*> once to skip the control variable option. When you are asked for a subset variable, choose **30** or **CLASS** with a minimum value of **1** (lower-class) and a maximum value of **2** (working-class). When the table appears on your screen, *press* **C** (for Column percentages). This is how the results will look:

	WHITE	BLACK
OBEDIENT	34.2	47.3
THINK	65.8	52.7

The results indicate that whites (34.2 percent) are less likely than African Americans (47.3 percent) to stress obedience more than independent thinking. Based on Kohn's theory, we would explain these results by saying that African Americans have learned from social experience that they are more successful when they conform to social norms than when they express their individuality. In this case, life experiences associated with race are even more significant than those associated with social status.

Overall, we have seen considerable support for the central idea behind Kohn's theory: parents draw on their own learning for the values they wish to pass on to their children. For better or worse, the life experiences of one generation are reflected in the values of the next.

Now we will turn our attention to another topic related to childrearing—spanking. Is approval of spanking related to the values parents believe their children should be taught? Are some of the socioeconomic factors we have examined thus far also related to the ways parents believe children should be disciplined? You will be able to answer those questions after you complete the exercises in the next section. Now it's your turn.

Other References

Kohn, Melvin. 1959. "Social Class and Parental Values," *American Journal of Sociology*, 64:337–351.

Kohn, Melvin, and Carmi Schooler. 1969. "Class, Occupation, and Orientation," *American Sociological Review*, 34:659–678.

----------------. 1983. *Work and Personality*. Norwood, NJ: Ablex.

Pearlin, L. I., and Melvin Kohn. 1966. "Social Class, Occupation, and Parental Values: A Cross-National Study," *American Sociological Review*, 31:466–479.

WORKSHEET

NAME:

COURSE:

DATE:

EXERCISE 12

If you have not already done so, open the **NORC** data file.

1. Go to the **Univariate Statistics** function and select variable **24) SPANK KIDS**. *Type* **D** (for Distribution) and read the survey question at the top of the screen. Fill in the table.

	FREQUENCY	%
AGREE		
DISAGREE		

How would you answer this question? (circle one)   Agree   Disagree

2. Return to the **STATISTICAL ANALYSIS MENU**. Select **B. Tabular Statistics**. Create and fill in the table below. Row variable: **24** or **SPANK KIDS**; column variable: **21** or **KID OBEY**. Remember to *press* **C** (for Column percentages).

	OBEDIENT	THINK
AGREE	%	%
DISAGREE	%	%

Prob. = _____

V = _____

Is the difference statistically significant? (circle one)   Yes   No

In light of these results, and of the research by Kohn that was presented in the introduction, how might social class be related to approval of spanking?

3. Create and fill in the table below. Row variable: **24** or **SPANK KIDS**; column variable: **30** or **CLASS**. Remember to use column percentaging.

	LOWER	WORKING	MIDDLE	UPPER
AGREE	%	%	%	%
DISAGREE	%	%	%	%

Prob. = _____

V = _____

Is the difference statistically significant? (circle one)   Yes   No

Were these the results you expected? Explain.

4. The hypothesis is: **Men will be more likely than women to approve of spanking as a form of discipline.**

   Make **24** or **SPANK KIDS** the row variable and **1** or **SEX** the column variable. Percentage the final results and fill in the table.

	MALE	FEMALE
AGREE	%	%
DISAGREE	%	%

Prob. = _____

V = _____

Is the difference statistically significant? (circle one)   Yes   No

Is the hypothesis supported or rejected? (circle one)   Supported   Rejected

How would you explain the relationship between gender and approval of spanking?

5. Make **24** or **SPANK KIDS** the row variable and **49** or **CH.ATTEND** the column variable. Percentage the final results and fill in the table.

	LESS OFTEN	ANNUALLY	MONTHLY	WEEKLY
AGREE	%	%	%	%
DISAGREE	%	%	%	%

Prob. = _____

V = _____

Is the difference statistically significant? (circle one)   Yes   No

Again, use **24** or **SPANK KIDS** as the row variable, but use **52** or **R.FUND/LIB** as the column variable. (If you don't recall the complete description of **R.FUND/LIB**, use **F3** to examine the description.) Percentage the final results and fill in the table.

	FUNDAMENT.	MODERATE	LIBERAL
AGREE	%	%	%
DISAGREE	%	%	%

Prob. = _____

V = _____

Is the difference statistically significant? (circle one)   Yes   No

Summarize the relationship between religion and attitudes toward spanking and then explain why you think these results occur.

6. The hypothesis is: **People who have no children will be less likely than those with children to approve of spanking as a form of discipline.**

   Make **24** or **SPANK KIDS** the row variable and **13** or **# CHILDREN** the column variable. Percentage the final results and fill in the table.

	NONE	1–2	3 OR MORE
AGREE	%	%	%
DISAGREE	%	%	%

Prob. = _____

V = _____

Is the difference statistically significant? (circle one)   Yes   No

Is the hypothesis supported or rejected? (circle one)   Supported   Rejected

Summarize the results of this analysis in one or two sentences. Why do you think these results occur?

7. Now it's time to test your own hypothesis. Remember, you can use **F3** to view and select variables, or you can consult the list of variables in the back of your book and type in the name or number of the variable you wish to select.

Write a hypothesis using the independent variable (cause) of your choice and **24) SPANK KIDS**, or another parenting related variable, as the dependent variable (effect):

_____

_____

Make **24** or **SPANK KIDS** the row, or dependent, variable.

What is your independent variable?   _____
(make this your column variable)

Type **C** (for Column percentages). *Press* **P** (for Print). (**Note:** If your computer is not connected to a printer, or you have been instructed not to use the printer, skip these printing instructions. Instead, draw a table on a separate sheet of paper showing the final, percentaged results.) Attach a copy of the results.

Is the difference statistically significant? (circle one)   Yes   No

Is the hypothesis supported or rejected? (circle one)   Supported   Rejected

Discuss why you think your hypothesis was, or was not, supported.

◆ CHAPTER 13 ◆

Families and Education:
An Introduction to Multiple Regression

Family and education have always been closely linked. Before 1642, when the Massachusetts colony passed the first mandatory school attendance law in the U.S., children received most of their training in the home. The extent of the training children received, whether it was reading and writing or just the learning of a trade, varied by historical period, geography, and social class—but prior to industrialization, the idea of *going to school* was reserved for a privileged few.

The formal shift of the responsibility for education occurred in 1954 in *Brown v. Board of Education*, when the Supreme Court ruled that education is a constitutional right that must be guaranteed by the state. So where does the family now fit in? Who has the most influence over a child's education—the family or school? In 1966, sociologist James S. Coleman found that it was the quality and structure of the family, more than the quality and structure of the school, which determined the outcome of a child's education.[1] Over thirty years have now passed since Coleman's research. Many changes have taken place both in schools and in the family. But as we shall see in this exercise, today's family is still very influential when it comes to education.

Start MicroCase, open the **STATES** data file, and go to **E. Mapping Variables** on the **STATISTICAL ANALYSIS MENU**. When you are asked for the name or number of the variable you wish to map, *type* **58** or **VERBAL SAT** and *press <ENTER>*. This is how the map will look:

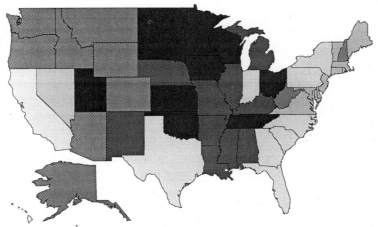

1992: Verbal Score on SAT

Most of the states with the highest scores on the verbal section of the SAT (Scholastic Aptitude Test) are located in the north central states. The lowest states are in the South and along portions of each coast. *Type* **D** (for Distribution). Ohio (545) has the highest scores, followed by Iowa (520) and North Dakota (518). The lowest scores are in South Carolina (396) and Georgia (399). Let's see if the distribution is similar for the scores on the math section of the SAT. Return to the map

---

[1] Coleman, James S., et al., 1966. *Equality of Educational Opportunities*. Washington, D.C.: U.S. Government Printing Office.

by *pressing* **A** (for Area map) or simply by *pressing* *<ENTER>*. *Type* **C** (for Compare). When you are asked for the name or number of the variable you wish to use for comparison, *type* **59** or **MATH SAT** and *press* *<ENTER>*.

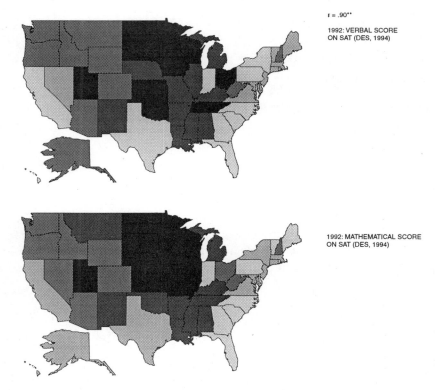

r = .90**

1992: VERBAL SCORE
ON SAT (DES, 1994)

1992: MATHEMATICAL SCORE
ON SAT (DES, 1994)

The maps are strikingly similar. In fact, the correlation coefficient (r) is 0.90, which means the rankings are nearly identical.

We need to examine one more SAT-related variable before we can try to explain variations in SAT scores. That is the percentage of high school graduates in each state who take the SAT. Not all states encourage their schools to use the SAT. Some may recommend a different test; others may discourage standardized testing altogether. *Press* *<ENTER>* once to clear the second map. This time, use **60** or **% TAK.SAT** as the comparison variable.

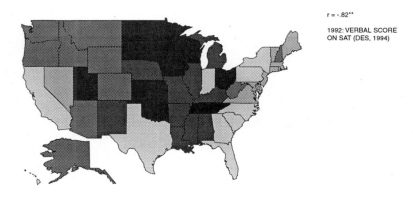

r = -.82**

1992: VERBAL SCORE
ON SAT (DES, 1994)

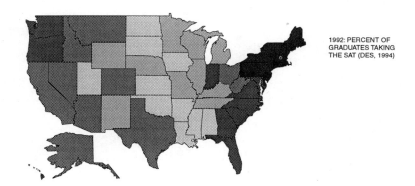

1992: PERCENT OF
GRADUATES TAKING
THE SAT (DES, 1994)

The states with the most students taking the exam are clearly not the states with the highest scores. The strong negative correlation (r = –0.82) tells us that the higher the percentage who take the test, the lower the average test score. It would appear that in those states that do not encourage its use, only the students who are likely to do well on the test are likely to take it. We will come back to the impact of this phenomenon in just a moment, but first let's look at some school-related variables that may affect SAT scores.

Press <ENTER> until you return to the **STATISTICAL ANALYSIS MENU**. Place the highlight on **G. Correlations** and *press <ENTER>*. When you are asked for the first variable, enter **58** or **VERBAL SAT**. Then enter the following variables: **54** or **PUPIL/TCH**, **55** or **$PER PUPIL**, and **56** or **TEACHER$**. *Press <ENTER>* twice to skip the subset option. Here are the results:

	58) VERBAL SAT	54) PUPIL/TCH	55) $PER PUPIL	56) TEACHER$
58) VERBAL SAT	—	0.028	–0.424**	–0.443**
54) PUPIL/TCH	0.028	—	–0.447**	–0.105
55) $PER PUPIL	–0.424**	–0.447**	—	0.856**
56) TEACHER$	–0.443**	–0.105	0.856**	—

Two of the variables have a statistically significant relationship with verbal SAT scores—the amount of money spent per pupil (–0.424) and teacher salaries (–0.433). But both correlations are negative! The more money the government spends on education, and the more pay teachers receive—the lower the SAT scores. What is going on here?

Think back to the map comparison of SAT scores with the percentage taking the SAT test. It was a negative correlation (r = –0.82); the more students who took the test, the lower the average score. What if the states that spend the most on education are the same states where most of the students take the SAT? Then those states will have lower SAT scores, not because of spending, but because they have more students taking the exam.

Press <ENTER> to clear the screen for another correlation matrix. Enter the following variables: **60** or **%TAK.SAT**, **55** or **$PER PUPIL**, and **56** or **TEACHER$**. *Press <ENTER>* to skip the subset option.

	60) %TAK.SAT	55) $PER PUPIL	56) TEACHER$
60) %TAK.SAT	—	0.681**	0.606**
55) $PER PUPIL	0.681**	—	0.856**
56) TEACHER$	0.606**	0.856**	—

Just as we might have suspected, there is a strong positive correlation between the percentage taking the SAT and spending per pupil (r = 0.681) and teacher salaries (r = 0.606). The states that spend the most money on education are the same ones that encourage taking the SAT. But how can we be sure which of these variables is actually having the negative impact on SAT scores? Maybe funding somehow does have a negative effect on school performance. Fortunately, social scientists have a technique for sorting out the impact of more than one variable at a time. It is called **multiple regression**.

Return to the main menu, place the highlight on **I. Regression**, and *press <ENTER>*. You are asked for the name or number of the dependent variable. In this instance, the variable we wish to explain, the one we think of as being caused, is the SAT scores. So *type* **58** or **VERBAL SAT** and *press <ENTER>*. You are now asked for the name or number of the first independent variable. *Type* **55** or **$PER PUPIL** and *press <ENTER>*. When you are asked for the name or number of the second independent variable, type **56** or **TEACHER$** and *press <ENTER>*. When you are asked for the name or number of the third independent variable, type **60** or **%TAK.SAT** and *press <ENTER>*. When you are asked for the name or number of a fourth independent variable, type nothing; simply *press <ENTER>*. *Press <ENTER>* again. This graphic will appear on the screen:

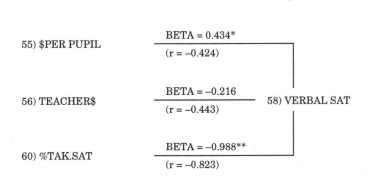

R-SQ = 0.725

55) $PER PUPIL   BETA = 0.434*   (r = –0.424)

56) TEACHER$ BETA = –0.216   (r = –0.443)   58) VERBAL SAT

60) %TAK.SAT   BETA = –0.988**   (r = –0.823)

In the upper right-hand corner, the screen reads: R-SQ = 0.725. This stands for R^2, which is **a measure of the combined effects** of the three independent variables on the dependent variable. In plain English, this means that the variables spending per pupil, teacher salaries, and the percentage of students taking the SAT together account for 72.5 percent of the variation in SAT scores (move the decimal to the right two digits to convert it to a percentage). Put another way, if all states spent the same amount on education and had the same percentage of students taking the test, there would have been 72.5 percent less variation in the average SAT scores.

But that's not all we can see in this graphic. Beneath each of the horizontal lines is the value of r, which is Pearson's correlation coefficient. These are, of course, the same values as those shown in the set of correlations we have already examined. Above each line is the word **BETA**, followed by a numerical value. This stands for the standardized beta, which estimates **the independent effect of each independent variable on the dependent variable.**

The independent variables in this analysis are correlated with one another as well as with the dependent variable. What regression does is sort out the independent contributions of these three variables. Reading from the top of the graphic down, what we first discover is that spending per pupil does not have a negative effect on SAT scores. We know this because its BETA is positive. Furthermore, the positive impact of spending per pupil on SAT scores is statistically significant, as indicated by the asterisk. One asterisk indicates significance at the .05 level; two asterisks indicate significance at the .01 level. Thus, per-pupil spending actually increases test scores (BETA = .434). As for teacher salaries, they have no statistically significant impact one way or the other (BETA = −.216). On the other hand, the percentage of students taking the SAT actually does have a negative relationship with average scores (BETA = −.988). Unlike the case with the variables related to spending on education, in this case, the correlation by itself was fairly accurate.

The negative correlation between the salaries of teachers and SAT scores is an example of a **spurious correlation**. Spurious correlations occur between two variables because each is related to some unexamined additional variable or variables. When this variable or set of variables is taken into account, spurious correlations disappear. In this case, the spurious correlation occurred because both **TEACHER$** and **VERBAL SAT** were related to the percentage of students taking the SAT. Once the variable **%TAK.SAT** was included in the analysis, the relationship between the salaries of teachers and SAT scores was no longer statistically significant—thus, it was a spurious, or false, correlation. The spurious correlation was caused by the fact that states that spend more on teacher salaries also have more students taking the SAT.

Let's use multiple regression to see how some family-related variables affect SAT scores. According to Coleman we would expect that **states that have more children living with their married parents should have higher SAT scores and states that have more families living below the poverty line should have lower SAT scores.** *Press <ENTER>* to clear the screen. Again, when you are asked for the name or number of the dependent variable, *type* **58** or **VERBAL SAT** and *press <ENTER>*. This time, use **46** or **%POOR.FAM** and **29** or **COU.CHLD** (which represents the percentage of households in each state occupied by a married couple and their own children) as the first two independent variables. Since we have already learned that states with high percentages of students who take the SAT has a strong effect on SAT scores, we'll want to continue to control for this variable. So, select **60** or **%TAK.SAT** as the third independent variable. Here is how the results will look:

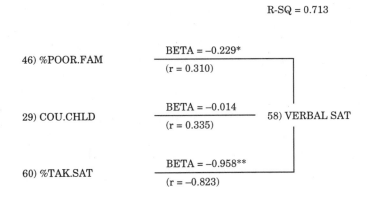

R-SQ = 0.713

46) %POOR.FAM — BETA = −0.229* (r = 0.310)

29) COU.CHLD — BETA = −0.014 (r = 0.335) — 58) VERBAL SAT

60) %TAK.SAT — BETA = −0.958** (r = −0.823)

Our hypothesis is partially supported. The percentage of families living below the poverty line is related to SAT scores (BETA = −0.229); the more poor families there are, the lower the average SAT score. However, the percentage of children living with their married parents does not appear to affect SAT scores. Although the *correlation* is moderately strong (r = 0.335), the relationship virtually disappears when the impact of the other variables is included (BETA = −0.014). This is another example of a spurious correlation. At least at the state level, the percentage of poor families in a state is a better predictor of that state's SAT scores than is the number of two-parent households. The fact that a state has more two-parent families does not guarantee that it will have higher average scores on the SAT.

Let's explore this point a little further by focusing on single-parent families. Does either the number of divorces or the number of single-parent families affect SAT scores? *Press <ENTER>* to clear the screen. Continue to use **58** or **VERBAL SAT** as the dependent variable. This time, use **40** or **DIVORCE 89, 36** or **%FEM.HEAD**, and **60** or **%TAK.SAT** as the independent variables. Here are the results:

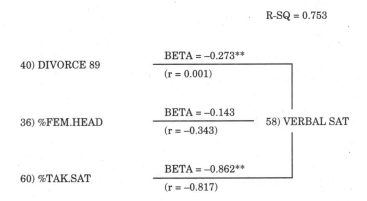

What we find is that the percentage of female-headed households is not related to SAT scores in a statistically significant manner (BETA = –0.143); however, the divorce rate has a statistically significant effect (BETA = –0.273). The higher the divorce rate, the lower the SAT scores. Using state-level data, we cannot tell whether those who took the SAT test lived in single-parent families or in families going through a divorce. But we can see that a state's divorce rate in a given year has more of an effect on SAT scores than does the percentage of single-parent families.

So far, our dependent variable has been scores on the SAT, which is a test most students take as they are completing high school. Would these findings be different if we looked at younger children—for example, eighth graders? Let's see how some of these same variables affect the scores on a math proficiency test given to students in the eighth grade. *Press <ENTER>* to clear the screen. This time, use **57** or **MATH SCORE** as the dependent variable. For your independent variables, use **40** or **DIVORCE 89, 36** or **%FEM.HEAD**, and **46** or **%POOR.FAM**. Here are the results:

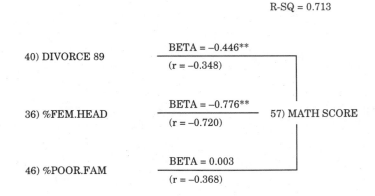

The results here are quite different from those we saw when we used SAT scores as the dependent variable. Here, both the percentage of female-headed homes (BETA = –0.776) and the divorce rate (BETA = –0.446) are statistically significant. The relationship between the percentage of families below the poverty line and math proficiency scores is not statistically significant (BETA = 0.003). Together, these variables account for 71 percent of the variation in math proficiency scores (R-SQ = 0.713). Again, we cannot assume that the students with the lowest math scores are necessarily living in single-parent families, but eighth-grade math scores in communities that have a higher divorce rate and more female-headed homes do tend to be lower overall.

One of the most difficult aspects of being a single parent is task overload—there is simply too much to do and not enough time. Work schedules and maintaining a household single-handedly can cut into time that single parents may want to devote to their children. Of course, many children in two-parent households are unsupervised to about the same extent. But it is easier for parents in two-parent households to find time to devote to parenting. One indirect measure of parental interaction in a community is the amount of time the kids who live there spend watching television. Communities in which the children are supervised less will generally watch more television. By including this variable in a regression, along with measures of family structure, we can separate the effects of supervision from other aspects of family structure. *Press <ENTER>* to clear the screen. Again, use **57** or **MATH SCORE** as the dependent variable. For your independent variables, use **36** or **%FEM.HEAD**, **46** or **%POOR.FAM**, and **81** or **TV>6HRS**. Here are the results:

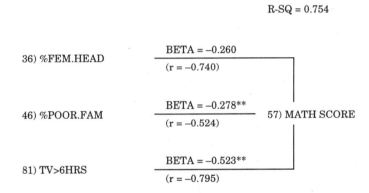

R-SQ = 0.754

| 36) %FEM.HEAD | BETA = –0.260 |
| | (r = –0.740) |

| 46) %POOR.FAM | BETA = –0.278** | 57) MATH SCORE |
| | (r = –0.524) |

| 81) TV>6HRS | BETA = –0.523** |
| | (r = –0.795) |

The percentage of children who watch more than six hours of television per day does indeed have a statistically significant negative effect on math scores (BETA = –0.523). In fact, this variable explains most of the effect of single parent households on math scores (BETA = –0.260). Communities in which children watch more television tend to have lower math scores overall.

What we have seen is that the relationship among schools, family, and academic achievement is very complex. There are no simple answers as to why some children do better at school than others, and there are no quick avenues to ensuring academic success. In the exercises that follow, you will have the opportunity to use multiple regression to examine some other education- and family-related issues that can be equally challenging to families and to society.

1. Open the **STATES** data set and select **G. Correlations**. Use the following list of variables to fill in the table below: **52, 54, 55,** and **56**.

	52) DROPOUTS	54) PUPIL/TCH	55) $PER PUPIL	56) TEACHER$
52) DROPOUTS				
54) PUPIL/TCH				
55) $PER PUPIL				
56) TEACHER$				

What is the correlation between **$PER PUPIL** and the dropout rate?   _____

Is the correlation statistically significant? (circle one)   Yes   No

What is the correlation between **TEACHER$** and the dropout rate?   _____

Is the correlation statistically significant? (circle one)   Yes   No

What is the correlation between **PUPIL/TCH** and the dropout rate?   _____

Is the correlation statistically significant? (circle one)   Yes   No

How would you explain these results?

2. *Press <ENTER>* until you return to the **STATISTICAL ANALYSIS MENU**. Select **I. Regression**. Before doing the following regression analysis, use **F3** to examine the variable descriptions for **54) PUPIL/TCH**, **9) %URBAN**, **55) $PER PUPIL**, and **14) AGE 5–17**. When you are finished, select **54** or **PUPIL/TCH** as your dependent variable. When you are asked for the independent variables, select variables **9**, **55**, and **14**. In the table below, fill in the correlation, beta, and R-SQ results.

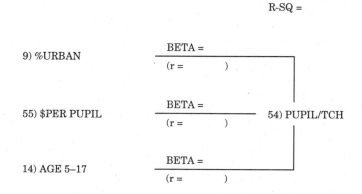

What is the explained variance (the combined effect) of these three independent variables (R-SQ)? (Remember to convert your decimal value to a percentage.)   _____ %

What is the independent or net effect of **%URBAN**?   _____

Is this BETA significant? (circle one)   Yes   No

What is the independent or net effect of **$PER PUPIL**?   _____

Is this BETA significant? (circle one)   Yes   No

What is the independent or net effect of **AGE 5–17**?   _____

Is this BETA significant? (circle one)   Yes   No

Summarize the results of this analysis in one or two sentences. Based on these results, where would you expect to find the most crowded classrooms?

3. *Press <ENTER>* to clear the regression results. Again use **F3** to examine **31) BOTH PARNT** and **87) LIBRARY**. Then select **52) DROPOUTS** as the dependent variable. When you are asked for the independent variables, select **31** or **BOTH PARNT** and **87** or **LIBRARY**. In the table below, fill in the correlation, beta, and R-SQ results.

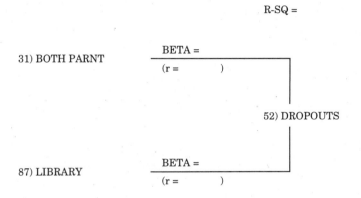

What is the explained variance (the combined effect) of these two independent variables (R-SQ)? (Remember to convert your decimal value to a percentage.)   _____ %

What is the independent or net effect of **BOTH PARNT**?   _____

Is this BETA significant? (circle one)   Yes   No

What is the independent or net effect of **LIBRARY**?   _____

Is this BETA significant? (circle one)   Yes   No

Summarize the results of this analysis in one or two sentences (**Note:** Look for differences between the correlation coefficient (r) and the BETA for each variable.) Then explain why you think these results occur.

4. *Press <ENTER>* to clear the regression screen. Again, use **F3** to examine each of the descriptions for the variables used in the following analysis. Then when you are asked for the name or number of the dependent variable, *type* **52** or **DROPOUTS** and *press <ENTER>*. When you are asked for the independent variables, select **31** or **BOTH PARNT**, **54** or **PUPIL/TCH**, and **2** or **SOUTHNESS**. In the table below, fill in the correlation, beta, and R-SQ results.

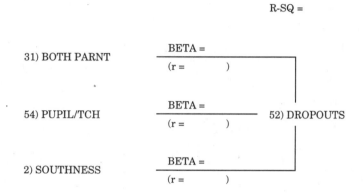

R-SQ =

31) BOTH PARNT   BETA =   (r =   )

54) PUPIL/TCH   BETA =   (r =   )   52) DROPOUTS

2) SOUTHNESS   BETA =   (r =   )

What is the explained variance (the combined effect) of these three independent variables (R-SQ)? (Remember to convert your decimal value to a percentage.) _____ %

What is the independent or net effect of **BOTH PARNT**? _____

Is this BETA significant? (circle one)   Yes   No

What is the independent or net effect of **PUPIL/TCH**? _____

Is this BETA significant? (circle one)   Yes   No

What is the independent or net effect of **SOUTHNESS**? _____

Is this BETA significant? (circle one)   Yes   No

Which of the variables above has the greatest effect on dropout rates? How would you explain these results?

5. Now it's time to test your own hypothesis. Remember, you can use **F3** to view and select variables, or you can consult the list of variables in the back of your book and type in the name or number of the variable you wish to select.

    Write a hypothesis using **52** or **DROPOUTS** as the dependent variable and two independent variables that you think will influence the dropout rate:

    _____

    _____

    What is your first independent variable?   _____

    What is your second independent variable?   _____

    When the graph is on your screen, *press* **P** (for Print). (**Note:** If your computer is not connected to a printer, or you have been instructed not to use the printer, skip these printing instructions. Instead, draw a diagram on a separate sheet of paper showing the final results.) Attach a copy of the results.

    What is the explained variance (the combined effect) of these two
    independent variables (R-SQ)? (Remember to convert your decimal
    value to a percentage.)   _____ %

    What is the independent or net effect of your first independent variable?   _____

    Is this BETA significant? (circle one)   Yes   No

    What is the independent or net effect of your second
    independent variable?   _____

    Is this BETA significant? (circle one)   Yes   No

    Is the hypothesis supported or rejected? (circle one)   Supported   Rejected

    Discuss why you think your hypothesis was, or was not, supported.

◆ CHAPTER 14 ◆
Divorce Rates

If you ask people who are divorced why their separations occurred, most will probably talk about issues related to personal incompatibility—*he* was like this, *she* was like that. A study by Kitson and Sussman (1982) found that the four most common reasons given for divorce were, in descending order of frequency, personality problems, home life, authoritarianism, and differing values. All of these reasons focus on the characteristics of individuals rather than of society. But can we ignore the impact that a couple's social environment may have on their decision to divorce, especially when divorce rates vary from one region of the country to another? In this exercise, we will step back and look at divorce from a broader perspective. We will focus on the nature of the communities in which couples live rather than on the couples themselves.

Start MicroCase, open the **STATES** data file, and go to the **STATISTICAL ANALYSIS MENU**. Place the highlight on **E. Mapping Variables** and *press <ENTER>*. Now you are asked for the name or number of the variable you wish to map. Let's start by looking at the divorce rate in each of the 50 states. *Type* **40** or **DIVORCE 89** and *press <ENTER>*. A map appears, showing you the number of divorces per 1,000 people in each state.

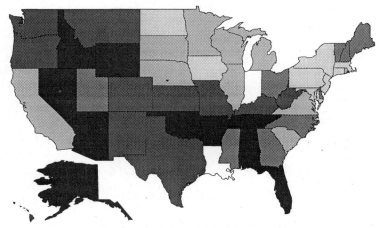

1989: Divorces per 1,000 population

Divorce rates do not vary randomly; there are distinct regional differences. The states with the highest divorce rates are located in the West and the South. *Type* **N** (for Name). A large arrow points to Nevada, and at the bottom left of the screen we see that there were 11.9 divorces for every 1,000 residents living there. *Type* **D** (for Distribution). Here we see that Oklahoma is distant second to Nevada, and then come Arkansas and Tennessee. Massachusetts had the lowest divorce rate (2.6 divorces per 1,000 residents) followed by Connecticut, Pennsylvania, and several other New England states. (Remember that states coded with –9999 mean that there is missing data.)

Have western and southern states always had the highest divorce rates? *Type* **A** (for Area map) to return to the map, then *type* **C** (for Compare). Now the map shrinks to half size and moves to the top of the screen. You are asked for the name or number of the variable for comparison. *Type* **96** or **DIVORCE 22** and *press <ENTER>*. A second map will appear.

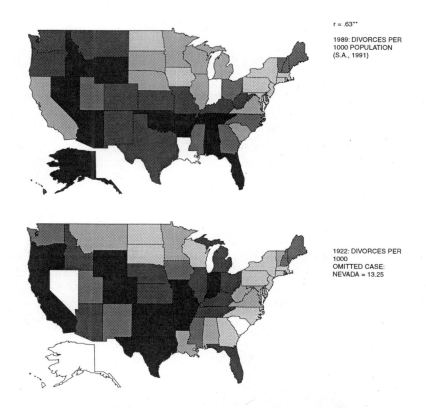

The maps are very similar, and the correlation coefficient at the upper right indicates a significant *positive* relationship of .63. The states that had higher divorce rates in 1989 also had higher divorce rates in 1922. These findings are interesting because they demonstrate that we must go beyond *personal incompatibility* in order to explain divorce. If divorce rates were *entirely* dependent on decisions made by autonomous individuals, divorce rates would be very unpredictable. States that had a high divorce rate one year would be no more or less likely to have a high divorce rate the following year. But the comparison of the divorce rates of 1922 with those of 1989 shows very little fluctuation. There must be something about living in the West or the South that increases the likelihood of divorce.

Let's compare the map of divorce rates with other maps to see if we can identify some possible reasons why some states have a higher divorce rate than others. We can begin with church membership. Because many churches discourage divorce, perhaps the variations in the divorce rates from region to region are related to the percentage of the population in each state who are members of a church. To check this out, *press <ENTER>* once to clear the lower map and use **61** or **CH.MEMBER** as the comparison map.

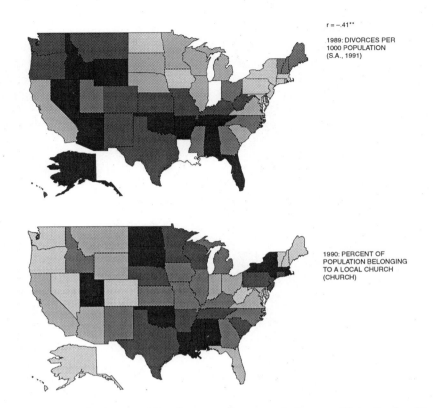

r = −.41**

1989: DIVORCES PER
1000 POPULATION
(S.A., 1991)

1990: PERCENT OF
POPULATION BELONGING
TO A LOCAL CHURCH
(CHURCH)

These maps are very different, as evidenced by the *negative* correlation coefficient of −.41. The divorce rates are higher in those states with fewer church members.

Another factor that may influence a state's divorce rate is education. A more educated population probably has the economic resources and/or the interpersonal skills that increase marital stability. *Press <ENTER>* once and use **53** or **% COLLEGE** as the comparison map. These maps are nearly mirror images of one another, as indicated by the *negative* relationship of −.40. The more college graduates there are in a state, the lower the divorce rate.

One last map comparison: *Press <ENTER>* once and select **6** or **NO MOVE** for the comparison map. Again, these maps are not very similar and there is a *negative* correlation coefficient (−.53). States that have more mobile populations also have higher divorce rates. This variable is a good indicator of social integration. People are generally more integrated into a community when there are fewer of the disruptions that result from people's moving in and out. So how does social integration influence the divorce rate? One explanation would be that long-term relationships with people in the community may diffuse some of the responsibility placed on marital relationships, thus making it easier for the marriage to survive. There are people around to meet the needs that spouses may not be able to meet by themselves. Another explanation would be that it is easier for couples to get divorced in communities where they feel more anonymous. There is more pressure to stay together in communities where everyone knows everyone else.

Thus far, we have used correlations to show how religion, education, and social integration are all related to the divorce rate. Now let's switch to multiple regression to explore these relationships further.

Press <ENTER> several times to return to the main menu and select **I. Regression**. You are asked for the name or number of the dependent variable. In this instance, the variable we wish to explain, the one we think of as being caused, is the divorce rate. So *type* **40** or **DIVORCE 89** and *press <ENTER>*. You are now asked for the name or number of the first independent variable. *Type* **53** or **% COLLEGE** and *press <ENTER>*. When you are asked for the name or number of the second independent variable, *type* **61** or **CH.MEMBER** and *press <ENTER>*. When you are asked for the name or number of a third independent variable, *type* **6** or **NO MOVE** and *press <ENTER>*. When you are asked for the name or number of a fourth independent variable, type nothing; simply *press <ENTER>*. *Press <ENTER>* again to skip the subset option. This graphic will appear on the screen:

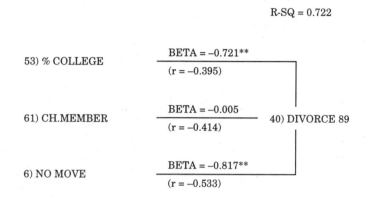

R-SQ = 0.722

53) % COLLEGE   BETA = –0.721**
         (r = –0.395)

61) CH.MEMBER   BETA = –0.005   40) DIVORCE 89
         (r = –0.414)

6) NO MOVE   BETA = –0.817**
         (r = –0.533)

In the upper right-hand corner, the screen reads: R-SQ = 0.722. This stands for R^2, which, as you may remember from Chapter 13, is a measure of the combined effects of the three independent variables on the dependent variable. In plain English, this means that church membership, the percentage of college graduates, and social integration together account for 72.2 percent of the variation in divorce rates among the states.

In addition to allowing us to look at the combined effects of the three independent variables, multivariate analysis lets us see the impact each independent variable analysis has on the dependent variable. In this case, we see that the percentage of college graduates and the percentage of non-movers are both related to the divorce rate. The BETA for **% COLLEGE** is –0.721. The BETA for **NO MOVE** is –0.817. The asterisks tell us that both BETAs are statistically significant at the .01 level. The more educated and the more socially integrated the population is, the lower the divorce rate.

Look now at the church membership variable. Although there is a correlation between church membership and the divorce rate (r = –0.414), when the influence of the other two independent variables is taken into account, the relationship between church membership and the divorce rate virtually disappears (BETA = –0.005). These results suggest that the relationship between church membership and the divorce rate is at least partly a result of the tendency for the church membership rates to be higher in those regions of the country that have less mobile populations. It could be that many people who become less religious and have not moved are still on the membership rolls of a church even if they quit attending the church or attend infrequently. This same population is not very likely to officially join a church if they move out of state. Thus, church membership rates are highly correlated with population stability. Another explanation could be that people are more likely to join a church in a community where they have long-term relationships with other people. In any event, the stability of the population has more of an influence on the divorce rate than does church membership.

Let's replace the more general church membership variable with a more specific religious variable. *Press <ENTER>* to clear these results. Again, use **40** or **DIVORCE 89** as the dependent variable and *press <ENTER>*. You are asked for the name or number of the first independent variable. *Type* **53** or **% COLLEGE** and *press <ENTER>*. You are asked for the name of the second independent variable. *Type* **63** or **% CATHOLIC** and *press <ENTER>*. When you are asked for the name or number of the third independent variable, *type* **6** or **NO MOVE** and *press <ENTER>*. When you are asked for the name or number of the fourth independent variable, type nothing; simply *press <ENTER>*. *Press <ENTER>* again. This graphic will appear on the screen:

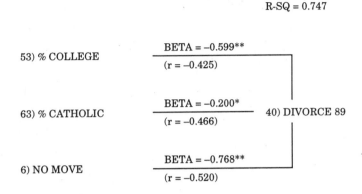

R-SQ = 0.747

53) % COLLEGE   BETA = −0.599**   (r = −0.425)

63) % CATHOLIC   BETA = −0.200*   (r = −0.466)   40) DIVORCE 89

6) NO MOVE   BETA = −0.768**   (r = −0.520)

The BETA for **% CATHOLIC** (−0.200) is not as large as that for **% COLLEGE** (−0.599) or **NO MOVE** (−0.768), but it is significant at the .05 level. So, although church membership is not related to the divorce rate when education and social mobility are controlled, the effect of Catholic church membership remains statistically significant when these same controls are added.

Let's take a closer look at the education variable. Education is highly correlated with income, so perhaps it is the higher income that comes with a college education, and not the education itself, that affects the divorce rate. *Press <ENTER>* to clear the screen. Again, use **40** or **DIVORCE 89** as the dependent variable and *press <ENTER>*. You are asked for the name or number of the first independent variable. *Type* **53** or **% COLLEGE** and *press <ENTER>*. You are asked for the name or number of the second independent variable. *Type* **45** or **MED.FAM $** and *press <ENTER>*. When you are asked for the name or number of a third independent variable, type nothing; simply *press <ENTER>*. *Press <ENTER>* again. This graphic will appear on the screen:

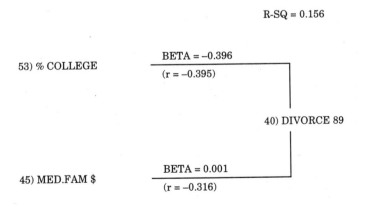

R-SQ = 0.156

53) % COLLEGE   BETA = −0.396   (r = −0.395)

40) DIVORCE 89

45) MED.FAM $ BETA = 0.001   (r = −0.316)

Although **MED.FAM $** is correlated with the divorce rate (r = −0.316), it retains no independent effect when the proportion of college graduates is controlled (BETA = 0.001). That is, most of the effect appears to be caused by the **% COLLEGE** variable. How might we interpret this? The results of developing an educated population go beyond the effects of money alone. Although the extra money college graduates earn probably does make family life easier to manage, a college education develops other skills that may lead to marital stability (e.g., improved communication and flexibility).

The results of the analyses we have looked at so far do not allow us to predict whether particular individuals are likely to divorce, but they do tell us something about the divorce rate overall. States that have educated, geographically stable populations tend to have lower divorce rates. In the regressions that follow, you will have the opportunity to examine some other factors that may affect the divorce rate.

Reference

Kitson, Gay, and Marvin Sussman. "Marital Complaints, Demographic Characteristics, and Symptoms of Mental Distress in Divorce." *Journal of Marriage and the Family*, 44:1 (1982) 87–101.

WORKSHEET

NAME: _____

COURSE: _____

DATE: _____

EXERCISE

14

1. Open the **STATES** data set and select the regression function. *Press* **F3** and examine the complete variable description for **16) % OVER 84**. Close these windows and select **40 or DIVORCE 89** as the dependent variable in the regression analysis. When you are asked for the independent variables, *type* **16 or % OVER 84** and **6 or NO MOVE**. *Press <ENTER>* to skip the subset option. Fill in the correlation, beta, and R-SQ values below.

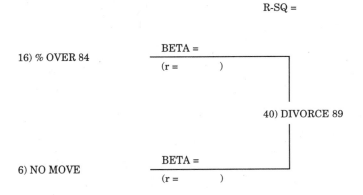

R-SQ = _____

16) % OVER 84

BETA = _____
(r = _____)

40) DIVORCE 89

6) NO MOVE

BETA = _____
(r = _____)

What is the explained variance (the combined effect) of these two independent variables (R-SQ)? (Remember to convert your decimal value to a percentage.) _____ %

What is the independent or net effect of **% OVER 84**? _____

Is this BETA significant? (circle one)   Yes   No

What is the independent or net effect of **NO MOVE**? _____

Is this BETA significant? (circle one)   Yes   No

Summarize the relationship between states with large populations over age 84 and the divorce rate. (**Note:** Look for differences between the correlation coefficient (r) and the BETA.) How do you think age and geographic mobility might be related?

WORKSHEET

2. *Press <ENTER>* to clear the screen. Before selecting variables for a new regression analysis, use **F3** to examine the complete variable descriptions for **29) COU.CHLD** and **30) COU.NO CH**. The hypothesis is: **States that have more married couples with children will have lower divorce rates, while states that have more couples without children will have higher divorce rates.** When you are asked for the name or number of the dependent variable, *type* **40** or **DIVORCE 89** and *press <ENTER>*. When you are asked for the independent variables, enter **29** or **COU.CHLD** and **30** or **COU.NO CH**. Fill in the results in the diagram below:

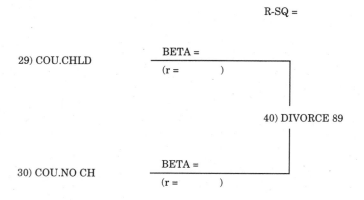

R-SQ =

29) COU.CHLD

BETA =

(r =   )

40) DIVORCE 89

30) COU.NO CH

BETA =

(r =   )

What is the explained variance (the combined effect) of these two independent variables (R-SQ)? (Remember to convert your decimal value to a percentage.) _____ %

What is the independent or net effect of **COU.CHLD**? _____

Is this BETA significant? (circle one)   Yes   No

What is the independent or net effect of **COU. NO CH**? _____

Is this BETA significant? (circle one)   Yes   No

Is the hypothesis supported or rejected? (circle one)   Supported   Rejected

Based on these results, what would you conclude about children and the divorce rate?

3. The hypothesis is: **States that are more urban and where use of cocaine is more prevalent will have higher rates of divorce.** When you are asked for the name or number of the dependent variable, *type* **40** or **DIVORCE 89** and *press <ENTER>*. When you are asked for the independent variables, select **66** or **COKE USERS** and **9** or **%URBAN** and *press <ENTER>* twice. Fill in the diagram below.

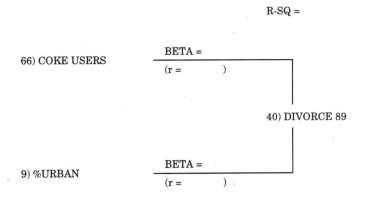

R-SQ =

66) COKE USERS   BETA = _____

                    (r =   )

                                            40) DIVORCE 89

9) %URBAN   BETA = _____

                    (r =   )

What is the explained variance (the combined effect) of these two independent variables (R-SQ)? (Remember to convert your decimal value to a percentage.)   _____ %

What is the independent or net effect of **COKE USERS**?   _____

Is this BETA significant? (circle one)   Yes   No

What is the independent or net effect of **%URBAN**?   _____

Is this BETA significant? (circle one)   Yes   No

Is the hypothesis supported or rejected? (circle one)   Supported   Rejected

Summarize the results of this analysis in one or two sentences. Then explain why you think these results occur.

4. The hypothesis is: **States where the residents drink more beer and wine will have higher divorce rates.** When you are asked for the name or number of the dependent variable, *type* **40** or **DIVORCE 89** and *press <ENTER>*. When you are asked for the independent variables, select **70** or **BEER** and **71** or **WINE**. Fill in the diagram below.

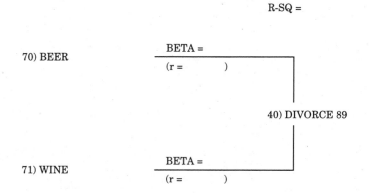

R-SQ =

70) BEER

BETA =

(r =   )

40) DIVORCE 89

71) WINE

BETA =

(r =   )

What is the explained variance (the combined effect) of these two independent variables (R-SQ)? (Remember to convert your decimal value to a percentage.) _____ %

What is the independent or net effect of **BEER**? _____

Is this BETA significant? (circle one)   Yes   No

What is the independent or net effect of **WINE**? _____

Is this BETA significant? (circle one)   Yes   No

Is the hypothesis supported or rejected? (circle one)   Supported   Rejected

How would you explain these results?

5. The hypothesis is: **States where the violent crime rates are high and states where the property crime rates are high will have higher divorce rates.** When you are asked for the name or number of the dependent variable, *type* **40** or **DIVORCE 89** and *press <ENTER>.* When you are asked for the independent variables, select **67** or **P.CRIME** and **68** or **V.CRIME**. Fill in the diagram below.

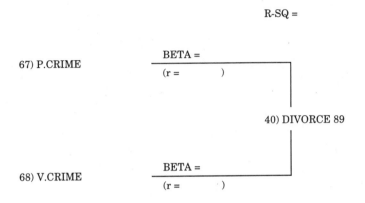

What is the explained variance (the combined effect) of these two independent variables (R-SQ)? (Remember to convert your decimal value to a percentage.)   _____ %

What is the independent or net effect of **V.CRIME**?   _____

Is this BETA significant? (circle one)   Yes   No

What is the independent or net effect of **P.CRIME**?   _____

Is this BETA significant? (circle one)   Yes   No

Repeat this analysis with the addition of a third variable. *Press <ENTER>* to clear the screen. When you are asked for the name or number of the dependent variable, *type* **40** or **DIVORCE 89** and *press <ENTER>*. When you are asked for the independent variables, select **67** or **P.CRIME**, **68** or **V.CRIME**, and **6** or **NO MOVE**. Fill in the diagram below.

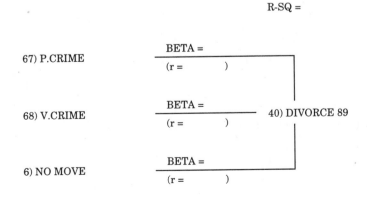

What is the explained variance (the combined effect) of these three independent variables (R-SQ)? (Remember to convert your decimal value to a percentage.)

_____ %

What is the independent or net effect of **V.CRIME**?

_____

Is this BETA significant? (circle one)

Yes   No

What is the independent or net effect of **P.CRIME**?

_____

Is this BETA significant? (circle one)

Yes   No

What is the independent or net effect of **NO MOVE**?

_____

Is this BETA significant? (circle one)

Yes   No

Is the hypothesis supported or rejected? (circle one)   Supported   Rejected

How would you explain the different results when **NO MOVE** is added?

6. The hypothesis is: **States that have more Baptists will have lower divorce rates, and states that have more people who are not religious will have higher divorce rates.** When you are asked for the name or number of the dependent variable, *type* **40** or **DIVORCE 89** and *press* *<ENTER>*. When you are asked for the independent variables, select **64** or **% BAPTIST** and **62** or **%NO RELIG**. Fill in the diagram below.

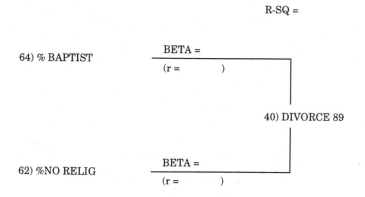

R-SQ =

64) % BAPTIST

BETA =

(r =   )

40) DIVORCE 89

62) %NO RELIG

BETA =

(r =   )

What is the explained variance (the combined effect) of these two independent variables (R-SQ)? (Remember to convert your decimal value to a percentage.)   _____ %

What is the independent or net effect of **% BAPTIST**?   _____

Is this BETA significant? (circle one)   Yes   No

What is the independent or net effect of **%NO RELIG**?   _____

Is this BETA significant? (circle one)   Yes   No

Is the hypothesis supported or rejected? (circle one)   Supported   Rejected

Were these the results you expected? Explain.

Create and fill in the graph below. When you are asked for the name or number of the dependent variable, *type* **40** or **DIVORCE 89** and *press <ENTER>*. When you are asked for the independent variables, select **64** or **% BAPTIST** and **53** or **% COLLEGE**.

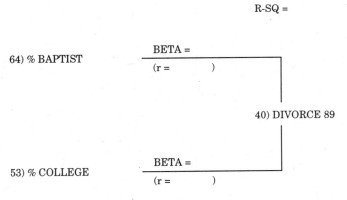

R-SQ =

64) % BAPTIST

BETA =
_____
(r =   )

40) DIVORCE 89

53) % COLLEGE

BETA =
_____
(r =   )

What is the explained variance (the combined effect) of these two independent variables (R-SQ)? (Remember to convert your decimal value to a percentage.)   _____ %

What is the independent or net effect of **% BAPTIST**?   _____

Is this BETA significant? (circle one)   Yes   No

What is the independent or net effect of **MED.FAM $**?   _____

Is this BETA significant? (circle one)   Yes   No

Based on the results, how would you summarize the relationship between Baptists and divorce? Explain.

7. Now it's time to test your own hypothesis. Remember, you can use **F3** to view and select variables, or you can consult the list of variables in the back of your book and type in the name or number of the variable you wish to select.

Write a hypothesis using **40** or **DIVORCE 89** as the dependent variable and two independent variables that you think will influence the divorce rate:

_____

_____

What is your first independent variable?   _____

What is your second independent variable?   _____

When the graph is on your screen, _press_ **P** (for Print). (**Note:** If your computer is not connected to a printer, or you have been instructed not to use the printer, skip these printing instructions. Instead, draw a diagram on a separate sheet of paper showing the final results.) Attach a copy of the results.

What is the explained variance (the combined effect) of these two independent variables (R-SQ)? (Remember to convert your decimal value to a percentage.)   _____ %

What is the independent or net effect of your first independent variable?   _____

Is this BETA significant? (circle one)   Yes   No

What is the independent or net effect of your second independent variable?   _____

Is this BETA significant? (circle one)   Yes   No

Is the hypothesis supported or rejected? (circle one)   Supported   Rejected

Discuss why you think your hypothesis was, or was not, supported.

◆ CHAPTER 15 ◆

The Divorced American

In this chapter, we will look at divorced Americans and see who they are and whether they differ from Americans who have not been divorced. Let's begin by looking at the current marital status of the entire sample. Open the **NORC** data file and go to **A. Univariate Statistics** on the **STATISTICAL ANALYSIS MENU**. When you are asked for the name or number of a variable to examine, *type* **4** or **MARITAL**. Skip the subset option by *pressing <ENTER>*. This pie chart shows the current marital status of everyone surveyed. *Type* **D** to look at the distribution.

	FREQUENCY	%
MARRIED	2400	52.2
WIDOWED	460	10.0
DIVORCED	676	14.7
SEPARATED	146	3.2
NEV.MARR.	914	19.9

Just over one half of the respondents are currently married. Those who are currently divorced make up the third largest category, at 15 percent. Of course, some of those who are currently married may have been divorced previously. To see how many people have ever been divorced, *press <ENTER>* twice and select **7** or **EVER DIVOR** as the new variable. The proportion of those who have ever divorced still represents a minority of the respondents. *Type* **D** (for Distribution).

	FREQUENCY	%
YES	853	26.3
NO	2388	73.7

Only 26.3% of those surveyed have ever been divorced. Undoubtedly you have heard or read that one half of all marriages end in divorce—so why is the number of divorced persons in this sample so low? First, we must remember how the popular "50 percent" statistic is computed. It is derived by dividing the number of divorces each year by the number of marriages. Recently, there has been one divorce for every two marriages—thus, one half of all marriages end in divorce. However, what this figure does not reflect is that some people marry and divorce more than once. Thus, although one half of all marriages may end in divorce, many fewer than one half of all married people will ever divorce.

Another factor that may account for the relatively low proportion of divorced persons in this survey is that a survey can measure only the present—not the future. Some of those who had never been divorced at the time these data were collected may divorce at a later time. One of the ways we can see this, as well as the increase in the divorce rate over time, is by examining the age-divorce relationship. *Press <ENTER>* until you return to the **STATISTICAL ANALYSIS MENU**. Go to **B. Tabular Statistics**. When you are asked for the name or number of the row variable, *type* **7** or **EVER DIVOR** and *press <ENTER>*. When you are asked for the name or number of the column variable, *type* **2** or **AGE** and *press <ENTER>*. *Press <ENTER>* two more times to skip the control variable and subset options. *Press* **C** (for Column percentages). These results will appear on your screen:

	18–29	30–39	40–49	50–64	65 & OVER
YES	13.7	24.1	36.6	33.2	18.9
NO	86.3	75.9	63.4	66.8	81.1

The results are somewhat complex, because two different processes are operating. First, the low proportion who have ever been divorced in the 65-and-over age group undoubtedly reflects a change over time in the proportion getting divorced. The low percentage for persons under 40 reflects, at least in part, that many of these marriages are still too new to have had a substantial opportunity to end in divorce—some of these people undoubtedly will get divorced in later years. However, recently there have been signs of a decline in divorce, so some of the differences across the younger two groups may also be reflecting a societal change.

Another age-related variable that we would expect to be related to divorce is the age at which a person weds. Because emotional and financial security increases with age, we would expect that **the younger people are when they marry, the more likely they are to divorce**. *Press <ENTER>* to clear the screen for a new table. This time, make **7** or **EVER DIVOR** the row variable and **6** or **AGE WED** the column variable. Skip the control and subset options and *press* **C** (for Column percentages). Your results will look like this:

	18 OR UNDE	19–20	21–22	23–25	OVER 25
YES	45.8	33.9	27.4	21.6	16.9
NO	54.2	66.1	72.6	78.4	83.1

The pattern is quite evident. The proportion of those who have been divorced is nearly three times higher for those who married at age 18 or younger (45.8 percent), by comparison with those who waited until they were past age 25 to marry (16.9 percent). *Press* **S** (for Statistics). The probability is 0.000; the hypothesis is supported.

One reason many young people delay marriage is so that they can pursue a college degree. Furthering one's education will ultimately benefit a marriage by providing financial security. The college experience also develops other skills that may enhance a marriage relationship, such as improved communication and an appreciation of other people's ways of seeing the world. Therefore, the hypothesis is: **Those who have completed college will be less likely to have divorced.** *Press <ENTER>* twice to clear the screen for a new table. Make **7** or **EVER DIVOR** the row variable and **42** or **DEGREE** the column variable. When the final table appears, *press* **C** (for Column percentages). Your results will look like this:

	NOT H.S.	HIGH SCH.	JR. COL.	B.A.	GRAD. DEG.
YES	26.1	29.4	31.1	18.6	18.1
NO	73.9	70.6	68.9	81.4	81.9

The results are consistent with the hypothesis. Reading across the top of the table, we find a noticeable drop in the proportion divorced when we get to those who have earned a college degree. For example, 29.4 percent of high school graduates have ever divorced, by comparison with 18.6 percent for those with a bachelor's degree from college. A look at the statistics will show that the difference is statistically significant (Prob. = 0.000). The hypothesis is supported.

Those who have less education will more than likely have lower incomes as well—which we would again expect to increase the likelihood of divorce by placing an additional strain on the marriage relationship. To demonstrate this, select **7** or **EVER DIVOR** as your row variable and **30** or **CLASS** as your column variable. When the final table appears, *press* **C** (for Column percentages). These results will appear on your screen:

	LOWER	WORKING	MIDDLE	UPPER
YES	30.1	30.5	22.8	21.2
NO	69.9	69.5	77.2	78.8

The highest percentages of persons who have ever been divorced are among those who identify themselves as being from the lower or working class. Of course, these low incomes can be a *result* of divorce as well, but research has shown that economic distress can lead to marital breakdown. When there is less money to spend, disagreements over financial matters become more frequent and the stress of living from paycheck to paycheck takes its toll over time.

Now let's take a look at religion. Does religious affiliation influence the probability of divorce? Make **7** or **EVER DIVOR** the row variable and **51** or **RELIGION** the column variable. When the final table appears, *press* **C** (for Column percentages). These results will appear on your screen:

	PROTESTANT	CATHOLIC	JEWISH	NONE
YES	27.8	19.4	26.1	36.6
NO	72.2	80.6	73.9	63.4

Overall, those who claim some type of religious affiliation are less likely to divorce than those who are not religious. The lowest proportion of divorced persons is among those who identify themselves as Catholic (19.4 percent). This is not surprising, since the Roman Catholic Church has traditionally had strong prohibitions against the dissolution of marriages except under special circumstances. Protestant (27.8 percent) and Jewish (26.1 percent) groups both have a lower percentage of divorced members than do those who claim no religious affiliation (36.6 percent).

Lastly, let's take a look at the impact of children on the likelihood of divorce. Do parents stay together for the sake of their children? To answer this question, select **8** or **DIV/MAR** as the row variable and **13** or **# CHILDREN** as the column variable. When the final table appears, *press* **C** (for Column percentages). Here are the results:

	NONE	1–2	3 OR MORE
MARRIED	73.0	74.4	75.3
DIVORCED/S	27.0	25.6	24.7

The difference between those who have children and those who do not is very slight. *Type* **S** (for Statistics). The probability is 0.645, which means the difference is not statistically significant. It appears that those marriages that are headed toward divorce will end up there whether or not children are involved. So children do not prevent divorce—but do they at least slow down the process? Maybe parents will wait at least until their children are older before they separate. Let's test this idea by using **8** or **DIV/MAR** as the row variable and **18** or **KIDS < 6** as the column variable. When the final table appears, *press* **C** (for Column percentages). Your results will look like this:

	NONE	1 OR MORE
MARRIED	72.1	83.4
DIVORCED/S	27.9	16.6

The difference here is a bit larger. Among those who have no children under the age of 6, 27.9 percent are divorced, compared to 16.6 percent for those who have one or more children under the age of 6. If you look at the statistics, you will see that this difference is statistically significant (Prob. = 0.000). This supports what is sometimes called the *braking hypothesis*, which states that children do not prevent divorce but that they do slow down the process.

So far, we have been looking at the factors that may increase the likelihood of divorce. In the exercises that follow, you will be asked to analyze lifestyle differences between those who are currently divorced and those who are currently married.

Your turn.

EXERCISE
15

If you have not already done so, open the **NORC** data file and go to the **Tabular Statistics** function.

1. The hypothesis is: **Those who are currently divorced, yet claim to have religion, will be less likely to attend a fundamentalist church.**

    If you do not recall the complete description for **52) R.FUND/LIB**, use **F3** to examine its variable description. Make **8** or **DIV/MAR** the row variable and **52** or **R.FUND/LIB** the column variable. Do not select a control or a subset variable. *Press* **C** (for Column percentages) and fill in the table.

	FUNDAMENT.	MODERATE	LIBERAL
MARRIED	%	%	%
DIVORCED/S	%	%	%

    Prob. = _____

    V = _____

    Is the difference statistically significant? (circle one)   Yes   No

    Is the hypothesis supported or rejected? (circle one)   Supported   Rejected

    How would you explain these results?

2. Women who are currently divorced likely understand the necessity of being able to obtain employment. So the hypothesis is: **Women who are currently divorced will be more likely to approve of married women being employed.**

    For the row variable, select **39** or **WOMEN WORK** and for the column variable, select **8** or **DIV/MAR**. When you are asked for a control variable, *press <ENTER>*. When you are asked for the name or number of the subset variable, *type* **1** or **SEX** and *press <ENTER>*. Enter **2** for both the minimum and the maximum value. This will limit the analysis to females. When the final table appears, *press* **C** (for Column percentages). Fill in the table below.

	MARRIED	DIVORCED/S
APPROVE	%	%
DISAPPROVE	%	%

Prob. = _____

V = _____

Is the difference statistically significant? (circle one)   Yes   No

Is the hypothesis supported or rejected? (circle one)   Supported   Rejected

How would you explain these results?

3. Make **58** or **HAPPY?** the row variable and **8** or **DIV/MAR** the column variable. When the final table appears, *press* **C** (for Column percentages). Fill in the table below.

	MARRIED	DIVORCED/S
VERY HAPPY	%	%
PRET.HAPPY	%	%
NOT TOO	%	%

Prob. = _____

V = _____

Is the difference statistically significant? (circle one)   Yes   No

Which variable do you believe is the cause and which do you believe is the effect? Explain your answer.

4. Now make **97** or **HEALTH** the row variable and **8** or **DIV/MAR** the column variable. Make sure to use column percentaging for the final table.

	MARRIED	DIVORCED/S
EXCELLENT	%	%
GOOD	%	%
FAIR	%	%
POOR	%	%

Prob. = _____

V = _____

Is the difference statistically significant? (circle one)   Yes   No

Do you think there is a cause-and-effect relationship between these variables? If so, which variable do you believe is the cause and which do you believe is the effect? If not, how do you explain the differences for those with fair or poor health?

WORKSHEET

5. Create and fill in the table below. Make **98** or **OVERDRINK** the row variable and **8** or **DIV/MAR** the column variable. Make sure to percentage the final table.

	MARRIED	DIVORCED/S
YES	%	%
NO	%	%

Prob. = _____

V = _____

Is the difference statistically significant? (circle one)   Yes   No

Which variable do you believe is the cause and which do you believe is the effect? Discuss. Explain your answer.

6. Now it's time to test your own hypothesis. Remember, you can use **F3** to view and select variables, or you can consult the list of variables in the back of your book and type in the name or number of the variable you wish to select.

Write a hypothesis using either **8) DIV/MAR** or **7) EVER DIVOR** as the independent (cause) or dependent (effect) variable:

_____

_____

What is your dependent variable?   _____
(make this your row variable)

What is your independent variable?   _____
(make this your column variable)

Type **C** (for Column percentages). *Press* **P** (for Print). (**Note:** If your computer is not connected to a printer, or you have been instructed not to use the printer, skip these printing instructions. Instead, draw a table on a separate sheet of paper showing the final, percentaged results.) Attach a copy of the results.

Is the difference statistically significant? (circle one)   Yes   No

Is the hypothesis supported or rejected? (circle one)   Supported   Rejected

Discuss why you think your hypothesis was, or was not, supported.

◆ CHAPTER 16 ◆

Remarriage

During this century, there has been an increase in the marriage pattern that social scientists refer to as *serial monogamy*. In contrast to monogamy, which is marriage to only one partner, serial monogamy refers to more than one marriage as when someone remarries after a divorce. The purpose of this exercise will be to examine the frequency and characteristics of remarriages.

Let's begin by taking a look at how often remarriage occurs following a divorce. Open the **NORC** data set and go to the **STATISTICAL ANALYSIS MENU**. Place the highlight on **A. Univariate Statistics** and *press <ENTER>*. When you are asked which variable you wish to examine, select **10** or **DIV/REMAR** and *press <ENTER>* twice. After the pie chart appears, *type* **T** (for Table). These data will appear:

	FREQUENCY	%
DIVORCED	676	55.7
REMARRIED	537	44.3

This table represents the current marital status of individuals who have ever been divorced. Forty-four percent of the respondents have remarried. Based on past trends, we would predict that eventually more than half of those who have divorced will remarry. One thing this trend tells us is that the rising divorce rate does not necessarily mean Americans are disillusioned with the *institution* of marriage. The disappointment appears to be with particular marriage relationships.

How do remarriages compare with first marriages? One could argue that remarriages will be happier, since people should be more aware of what they are looking for in a mate and have found someone who meets their current needs. On the other hand, first marriages may be happier because they have navigated the transitions that have pulled other relationships apart. Let's take a look to see which argument is supported.

Press <ENTER> until you get back to the **STATISTICAL ANALYSIS MENU**. Place the highlight on **B. Tabular Statistics** and *press <ENTER>*. When you are asked for a row variable, select **59** or **HAPPY.MAR?**. For your column variable, select **9** or **REMARRIAGE**. *Press <ENTER>* until the table appears on your screen, then *press* **C** (for Column percentages). Here are the results you will see:

	1 MARRIAGE	REMARRIAGE
LESS HAPPY	39.0	38.4
VERY HAPPY	61.0	61.6

It appears that neither argument is correct—the percentages of those who have had one marriage are nearly identical to the percentages of those who are remarried. *Type* **S** (for Statistics). Prob. = 0.804, so the slight differences you do see are not statistically significant. Remarriages are no more or less happy than first marriages.

Press <ENTER> twice to prepare for a new table. Perhaps there are other differences that we can identify. For example, because divorce is a departure from traditional norms, we could hypothesize that **those who are remarried will have less traditional gender-role attitudes than those who are in their first marriages.** To test this hypothesis, use variable **39** or **WOMEN WORK** as your row variable and **9** or **REMARRIAGE** as your column variable. When the table appears on your screen, *type* **C** (for Column percentages).

	1 MARRIAGE	REMARRIAGE
APPROVE	82.0	82.8
DISAPPROVE	18.0	17.2

Again, the percentages are virtually identical. Persons who have divorced and remarried are no more or less likely than those who have never divorced to approve of women's working outside the home. Although remarriages vary from the traditional norm of marrying for life, remarriages can be just as traditional as first marriages. Attitudes toward divorce and remarriage are not predictive of other family norms and values. People carry their traditional gender-role attitudes with them from one marriage relationship to another.

Although gender-role attitudes may not be different in remarriages, there may be differences in the actual structure of the household. For example, because remarriages often involve children from the previous marriages of one, or both, spouses, we might hypothesize that **persons who are remarried will have more people living in their households**. To test this hypothesis, use variable **17** or **HHOLD SIZE** as your row variable and **9** or **REMARRIAGE** as your column variable. When the table appears on your screen, *type* **C** (for Column percentages).

	1 MARRIAGE	REMARRIAGE
1–2	42.9	47.9
THREE	20.7	24.6
FOUR	24.1	16.2
FIVE	12.4	11.4

There appears to be a difference, but it is not in the direction we hypothesized. Remarriages are more likely to have only two members in the household and are less likely to have four- or five-member households than are first marriages. *Press* **S** (for Statistics) and you will see that the difference is statistically significant (Prob. = 0.000). The hypothesis is rejected. Although some reconstituted households may involve children from one or more previous marriages, overall, remarriages lead to smaller households.

So far, we have compared remarriages with first marriages and have found that remarriages are not very different from first marriages with regard to marital happiness and gender-role attitudes, but that they are slightly smaller with regard to household size. In the exercises that follow, we will turn our attention to comparing those who have remarried following a divorce with those who have not.

Your turn.

WORKSHEET

NAME:

COURSE:

DATE:

EXERCISE 16

If you have not already done so, open the **NORC** data file. Remember to use **F3** to examine the complete variable description of any variable you are not familiar with.

1. Use the **Tabular Statistics** function to create and fill in the table below. Make variable **10** or **DIV/REMAR** the row variable and **1** or **SEX** the column variable. When the table appears on the screen, *type* **C** (for Column percentages).

	MALE	FEMALE
DIVORCED	%	%
REMARRIED	%	%

Prob. = _____

V = _____

Is the difference statistically significant? (circle one)　　　　Yes　　No

Summarize the results of this table in one or two sentences. Then explain why you think these results occur.

2. Variable **40) HELP HUBBY** asked whether the respondent agrees with the statement that "it is more important for a wife to help her husband's career than to have one herself." Those agreeing with the statement would be said to have more traditional gender-role attitudes, whereas those disagreeing with the statement would be said to not have traditional gender-role attitudes.

The hypothesis is: **Divorced persons with more traditional gender-role attitudes will be more likely to remarry.**

Make variable **10** or **DIV/REMAR** the row variable and **40** or **HELP HUBBY** the column variable. When the table appears on the screen, *type* **C** (for Column percentages). Fill in the table below.

	STR.AGREE	AGREE	DISAGREE	STR.DISAG
DIVORCED	%	%	%	%
REMARRIED	%	%	%	%

Prob. = _____

V = _____

Is the difference statistically significant? (circle one)   Yes   No

Is the hypothesis supported or rejected? (circle one)   Supported   Rejected

Were these the results you expected? Explain.

3. The hypothesis is: **The more children divorced people have, the less likely they are to remarry.** Create and fill in the table below. Make variable **10** or **DIV/REMAR** the row variable and variable **13** or **# CHILDREN** the column variable. *Press* **C** (for Column percentages).

	NONE	1–2	3 OR MORE
DIVORCED	%	%	%
REMARRIED	%	%	%

Prob. = _____

V = _____

Is the difference statistically significant? (circle one)   Yes   No

Is the hypothesis supported or rejected? (circle one)   Supported   Rejected

Were these the results you expected? Explain.

4. Create and fill in the table below. Make variable **10** or **DIV/REMAR** the row variable and **30** or **CLASS** the column variable. When the table appears on the screen, *type* **C** (for Column percentages). Fill in the table below.

	LOWER	WORKING	MIDDLE	UPPER
DIVORCED	%	%	%	%
REMARRIED	%	%	%	%

Prob. = _____

V = _____

Is the difference statistically significant? (circle one)   Yes   No

Summarize the results of this table in one or two sentences. Then explain why you think these results occur.

5. Create and fill in the table below. Make variable **10** or **DIV/REMAR** the row variable and **3** or **WH/BLACK** the column variable. When you are asked for the name or number of the control variable, *type* **1** or **SEX**. Do not select a second control variable or subset. The first table that appears is for MALES only. *Press* **C** (for Column percentages).

MALES

	WHITE	BLACK
DIVORCED	%	%
REMARRIED	%	%

Prob. = _____

V = _____

Is the difference statistically significant? (circle one)   Yes   No

Press <ENTER> once to return to the table for males, and *press <ENTER>* again to view the table for females (this is indicated at the top left corner of the screen). *Press* **C** *(for Column percentages).*

FEMALES

	WHITE	BLACK
DIVORCED	%	%
REMARRIED	%	%

Prob. = _____

V = _____

Is the difference statistically significant? (circle one)   Yes   No

Summarize the results of these tables in one or two sentences. Then suggest an explanation for any difference between the results for men and the results for women.

6. Now it's time to test your own hypothesis as to how first marriages will differ from remarriages. Remember, you can use **F3** to view and select variables, or you can consult the list of variables in the back of your book and type in the name or number of the variable you wish to select.

Write a hypothesis using **9** or **REMARRIAGE** as the independent (cause) variable:

_____

_____

What is your dependent variable?   _____
(make this your row variable)

Make **9) REMARRIAGE** the column variable.

Type **C** (for Column percentages). *Press* **P** (for Print). (**Note:** If your computer is not connected to a printer, or you have been instructed not to use the printer, skip these printing instructions. Instead, draw a table on a separate sheet of paper showing the final, percentaged results.) Attach a copy of the results.

Explain why you think your hypothesis was supported or was not supported.

CODEBOOKS

◆ SHORT LABEL: NORC ◆

1) SEX
2) AGE
3) WH/BLACK
4) MARITAL
5) SINGLE/MAR
6) AGE WED
7) EVER DIVOR
8) DIV/MAR
9) REMARRIAGE
10) DIV/REMAR
11) DIV.EASY?
12) COHABIT
13) # CHILDREN
14) CHLDBR.AGE
15) IDEAL#KIDS
16) LIVE W KID
17) HHOLD SIZE
18) KIDS < 6
19) KID.NOFREE
20) KIDS JOY
21) KID OBEY
22) HELP OTHRS
23) WORK HARD
24) SPANK KIDS
25) FAM @ 16
26) # SIBS
27) SOC.KIN
28) FAM$ @16
29) MOVERS
30) CLASS
31) OWN HOME?
32) WORK STAT
33) MAR.F.WRK

34) FAM.WORK
35) INC.IMP
36) ACCOM.IMP
37) CHANGE $?
38) LIKE JOB?
39) WOMEN WORK
40) HELP HUBBY
41) STAY HOME
42) DEGREE
43) MATE DEGR.
44) DAD EDUC
45) MOM EDUC
46) SP.DAD.ED
47) SP.MOM.ED
48) ED.HOMOGAM
49) CH.ATTEND
50) HOW RELIG?
51) RELIGION
52) R.FUND/LIB
53) SP.FUND.
54) R.FUND@16
55) SP.FUND@16
56) REL HOMOG
57) R16HOMOG.
58) HAPPY?
59) HAPPY.MAR?
60) FREQ.SEX
61) EVER STRAY
62) FRIEND SEX
63) PICKUP SEX
64) PAID SEX?
65) TEEN SEX?
66) PREM.SEX

67) XMAR.SEX
68) PORN.MORAL
69) WHY.HSEX?
70) HOMO.SEX
71) SEX ED?
72) ABORT ANY
73) INTERMAR.?
74) CHLD.CARE
75) OBIG.HELP
76) EDUCATE $
77) REP/DEM
78) VOTE IN 92
79) EXECUTE?
80) MARIJUANA
81) VETERAN
82) IMP:MARRY
83) IMP:KIDS
84) IMP:FINAN
85) IMP:NOT DP
86) IMP:GOD
87) GO SPORT
88) GO MUSIC
89) CRAFTS
90) GARDEN
91) HUNT/FISH
92) SEE MOVIE
93) WATCH TV
94) CAMPING
95) MEMBERSHPS
96) LIFE EXCIT
97) HEALTH
98) OVERDRINK
99) EVER HIT?

◆ SHORT LABEL: NSC ◆

1) TWO-PARENT
2) FAMILY $
3) WH/BLACK
4) GENDER
5) ADOPTED
6) MOM.EDUC

7) DAD.EDUC
8) AGE.HOMOG
9) AGE-DIFF
10) GET ALONG
11) CLOSE.MOM
12) CLOSE.DAD

13) ACADEMICS
14) DEGREE
15) FRIENDS?
16) UNHAPPY
17) LOOKS
18) AGE.1.DATE

19) DATE.FREQ
20) DATE.RULES
21) AGE.1.MEN
22) AGE.1.SEX

23) BC 1 SEX
24) FORCED SEX
25) FRNDS SEX?
26) CH.ATTEND

27) NO TROUBLE
28) ACT QUICK
29) RUN AWAY?

◆ SHORT LABEL: STATES ◆

1) STATE NAME
2) SOUTHNESS
3) WESTNESS
4) WARM WINTR
5) POP GO 90
6) NO MOVE
7) % FOREIGN
8) DENSITY
9) %URBAN
10) %RURAL
11) AVG. AGE
12) % UNDER 5
13) % UNDER 18
14) AGE 5–17
15) % OVER 65
16) % OVER 84
17) SEX RATIO
18) %MALE
19) %FEMALE
20) % WHITE
21) % BLACK
22) % ASIAN
23) % HISPANIC
24) % NON-ENGL
25) %SINGLE
26) %SINGLE M
27) %SINGLE F
28) COUPLES
29) COU.CHLD
30) COU.NO CH
31) BOTH PARNT
32) %DIVORCED

33) %M.DIVORCE
34) %F.DIVORCE
35) %MALE.HEAD
36) %FEM.HEAD
37) ONE P.HH
38) HHOLD SIZE
39) MARRIAGE
40) DIVORCE 89
41) BIRTH
42) TEEN MOMS
43) ADOPTION
44) ABORTION
45) MED.FAM $
46) %POOR.FAM
47) %NURS.HOME
48) NEW HSE $
49) %FEM.WRK90
50) AVG TRAVEL
51) WORK HOME
52) DROPOUTS
53) % COLLEGE
54) PUPIL/TCH
55) $PER PUPIL
56) TEACHER$
57) MATH SCORE
58) VERBAL SAT
59) MATH SAT
60) %TAK.SAT
61) CH.MEMBER
62) %NO RELIG
63) % CATHOLIC
64) % BAPTIST

65) SUICIDE
66) COKE USERS
67) P.CRIME
68) V.CRIME
69) RAPE
70) BEER
71) WINE
72) SYPHILIS
73) AIDS
74) %CLINTON92
75) MDs
76) SHRINKS
77) %FEM MD
78) %FEM VET
79) VIET VETS
80) %LEGION
81) TV>6HRS
82) TV DISH
83) PLAYBOY
84) FLD&STREAM
85) PET$PER
86) MS.
87) LIBRARY
88) BOOK $ PER
89) HUNTING
90) FISHING
91) %FEM.WRK40
92) MEDIAN$ 40
93) MARRIAGE 40
94) F WAGES 20
95) %FEM.WRK20
96) DIVORCE 22

1) SEX
RESPONDENT'S SEX

2) AGE
RESPONDENT'S AGE (98 = DK; 99 = NoAns)

3) WH/BLACK
RESPONDENT'S RACE WHITE/BLACK

4) MARITAL
Are you currently — married, widowed, divorced, separated, or have you never been married?

5) SINGLE/MAR
SINGLE OR EVER MARRIED

6) AGE WED
How old were you when you first married?

7) EVER DIVOR
HAVE YOU EVER BEEN DIVORCED?

8) DIV/MAR
Are you currently — married or divorced/separated?

9) REMARRIAGE
First marriage or remarriage.

10) DIV/REMAR
MARITAL STATUS OF INDIVIDUALS WHO HAVE BEEN DIVORCED

11) DIV.EASY?
Should divorce in this country be easier or more difficult to obtain than it is now?

12) COHABIT
Did you live with your husband/wife before you got married?

13) # CHILDREN
How many children have you ever had? Please count all that were born alive at any time (including any you had from a previous marriage).

14) CHLDBR.AGE
How old were you when your first child was born?

15) IDEAL#KIDS
What do you think is the ideal number if children to have?

16) LIVE W KID
As you know, many older people share a home with their grown children. Do you think this is generally a good idea or a bad idea?

17) HHOLD SIZE
NUMBER OF HOUSEHOLD MEMBERS

18) KIDS <6
NUMBER OF MEMBERS UNDER 6

19) KID.NOFREE
Having children interferes too much with the freedom of parents—do you agree or disagree?

20) KIDS JOY
Watching children grow up is life's greatest joy—do you agree or disagree?

21) KID OBEY
Which of these would you say is more important in preparing children for life ... To be obedient or To think for themselves?

22) HELP OTHRS
How important do you believe it is for a child to learn to help others?

23) WORK HARD
How important do you believe it is for a child to learn to work hard?

24) SPANK KIDS
Do you (agree) or (disagree) that it is sometimes necessary to discipline a child with a good, hard spanking?

25) FAM @ 16
Were you living with both your own mother and father around the time you were 16?

26) # SIBS
How many brothers and sisters did you have? Please count those born alive, but no longer living, as well as those alive now. Also include step-brothers and step-sisters, and children adopted by your parents.

27) SOC.KIN
HOW OFTEN: Spend a social evening with relatives?

28) FAM$ @16
Thinking about the time when you were 16 years old, compared with American families in general then, would you say your family income was—far below average, below average, average, above average, or far above average?

29) MOVERS
When you were 16 years old, were you living in the same (city/town/county)?

30) CLASS?
If you were asked to use one of four names for your social class, which would you say you belong in: the lower class, the working class, the middle class, or the upper class?

31) OWN HOME?
(Do you/Does your family) own your (home/apartment), pay rent, or what?

32) WORK STAT
Last week were you working full time, part time, or keeping house?

33) MAR.F.WRK
MARRIED FEMALE'S WORK STATUS

34) FAM.WORK
Family Work Status

35) INC.IMP
IMPORTANCE? High income

36) ACCOM.IMP
IMPORTANCE? Work important and gives a feeling of accomplishment

37) CHANGE $?
During the last few years, has your financial situation been getting better, worse or has it stayed the same?

38) LIKE JOB?
On the whole, how satisfied are you with the work you do — would you say you are very satisfied, moderately satisfied, a little dissatisfied, or very dissatisfied?

39) WOMEN WORK
Do you approve or disapprove of a married woman earning money in business or industry if she has a husband capable of supporting her?

40) HELP HUBBY
It is more important for a wife to help her husband's career than to have one herself.

41) STAY HOME
It is much better for everyone involved if the man is the achiever outside the home and the woman takes care of the home and family.

42) DEGREE
HIGHEST EDUCATIONAL DEGREE EARNED BY RESPONDENT

43) MATE DEGR.
HIGHEST EDUCATIONAL DEGREE OF RESPONDENT'S SPOUSE

44) DAD EDUC
What is the highest grade in elementary school or high school that your father (or substitute father) finished and got credit for?

45) MOM EDUC
What is the highest grade in elementary school or high school that your mother (substitute mother) finished and got credit for?

46) SP.DAD.ED
What is the highest grade or year of regular school that your husband's/wife's father ever completed? (SPPAEDUC)

47) SP.MOM.ED
What is the highest grade or year of regular school that your (husband's/wife's) mother ever completed? (SPMAEDUC)

48) ED.HOMOGAM
Do the spouses have the same level of education?

49) CH.ATTEND
How often do you attend religious services?

50) HOW RELIG?
Would you call yourself a strong (PREFERENCE NAMED ELSEWHERE) or a not very strong (PREFERENCE NAMED ELSEWHERE)?

51) RELIGION
What is your religious preference? Is it Protestant, Catholic, Jewish, some other religion, or no religion?

52) R.FUND/LIB
FUNDAMENTALISM/LIBERALISM OF RESPONDENT'S RELIGION

53) SP.FUND.
FUNDAMENTALISM/LIBERALISM OF RELIGION OF SPOUSE

54) R.FUND@16
FUNDAMENTALISM/LIBERALISM OF RELIGION RESPONDENT RAISED IN

55) SP.FUND@16
FUNDAMENTALISM/LIBERALISM OF RELIGION SPOUSE RAISED IN

56) REL HOMOG
CURRENT RELIGIOUS HOMOGAMY

57) R16HOMOG.
Were the spouses raised in similar religions?

58) HAPPY?
Taken all together, how would you say things are these days — would you say that you are very happy, pretty happy, or not too happy?

59) HAPPY.MAR?
IF CURRENTLY MARRIED: Taking things all together, how would you describe your marriage? Would you say that your marriage is very happy, pretty happy, or not too happy?

60) FREQ.SEX
About how often did you have sex during the last 12 months?

61) EVER STRAY
Have you ever had sex with someone other than your husband or wife while you were married?

62) FRIEND SEX
If you had other partners, please indicate all categories that apply to them. A. Close personal friend

63) PICKUP SEX
If you had other sex partners, was it with a casual date or pick-up?

64) PAID SEX?
If you had other sex partners, was it a person you paid or paid you for sex?

65) TEEN SEX?
If a male and female in their early teens, say 14 to 16 years old, have sex relations before marriage do you think it is always wrong, almost always wrong, wrong only sometimes, or not wrong at all.

66) PREM.SEX
If a man and woman have sex relations before marriage, do you think it is always wrong, almost always wrong, wrong only sometimes, or not wrong at all?

67) XMAR.SEX
What is your opinion about a married person having sexual relations with someone other than the marriage partner — is it always wrong, almost always wrong, wrong only sometimes, or not wrong at all?

68) PORN.MORAL
Sexual materials lead to breakdown of morals?

69) WHY.HSEX?
Do you think being homosexual is something people choose to be, or do you think it is something they cannot change?

70) HOMO.SEX
Is homosexuality wrong?

71) SEX ED?
Would you be for or against sex education in the public schools?

72) ABORT ANY
LEGAL ABORTION: If the women wants it for any reason?

73) INTERMAR.?
Do you think there should be laws against marriages between (Negroes/blacks) and whites?

74) CHLD.CARE
Families should receive financial benefits for child care when both parents work—do you agree or disagree?

75) OBIG.HELP
Sometimes people are asked to make great sacrifices for others in their family . . . When someone is asked to give such care, is it their obligation to do so, or should they give care only if they really want to? (OBTOHELP)

76) EDUCATE $
Spending on improving the nation's education system

77) REP/DEM
Generally speaking, do you usually think of yourself as a Republican or a Democrat?

78) VOTE IN 92
IF VOTED: Did you vote for Clinton, Bush or Perot? (PRES92)

79) EXECUTE?
Do you favor or oppose the death penalty for persons convicted of murder?

80) MARIJUANA
Do you think the use of marijuana should be made legal or not?

81) VETERAN
Have you ever been on active duty for military training or service for two consecutive months or more? IF YES: What was your total time on active duty?

82) IMP:MARRY
HOW IMPORTANT TO YOU: Being married?

83) IMP:KIDS
HOW IMPORTANT TO YOU: Having children?

84) IMP:FINAN
HOW IMPORTANT TO YOU: Being financially secure?

85) IMP:NOT DP
HOW IMPORTANT TO YOU: Being self-sufficient and not having to depend on others?

86) IMP:GOD
HOW IMPORTANT TO YOU: Having faith in God?

87) GO SPORT
LAST 12 MONTHS DID YOU: Attend an amateur or professional sports event

88) GO MUSIC
LAST 12 MONTHS DID YOU: Go to a classical music or opera performance, not including school performances.

89) CRAFTS
LAST 12 MONTHS DID YOU: Make art or craft objects such as pottery, woodworking, quilts, or paintings.

90) GARDEN
LAST 12 MONTHS DID YOU: Grow vegetables, flowers, or shrubs in a garden.

91) HUNT/FISH
LAST 12 MONTHS DID YOU: Go hunting or fishing.

92) SEE MOVIE
LAST 12 MONTHS DID YOU: Go out to see a movie in a theater.

93) WATCH TV
On the average day, about how many hours do you personally watch television?

94) CAMPING
LAST 12 MONTHS DID YOU: Go camping, hiking, or canoeing.

95) MEMBERSHPS
Number of memberships

96) LIFE EXCIT
In general, do you find life exciting, pretty routine, or dull?

97) HEALTH
Would you say your own health, in general, is excellent, good, fair, or poor?

98) OVERDRINK
Do you sometimes drink more than you think you should?

99) EVER HIT?
Have you ever been punched or beaten by another person?

◆ LONG LABEL: NSC ◆

1) TWO-PARENT
1 OR 2 PARENT HOUSEHOLD (Respondent age 12–16)

2) FAMILY $
TOTAL FAMILY INCOME (Parents of child age 12–16)

3) WH/BLACK
RACE WHITE/BLACK

4) GENDER
DEFINITIVE GENDER

5) ADOPTED
Were you adopted by either of the parents who raised you? (Respondent age 17–21)

6) MOM.EDUC
HIGHEST GRADE MOTHER COMPLETED

7) DAD.EDUC
HIGHEST GRADE FATHER COMPLETED

8) AGE.HOMOG
Difference in age between married mother and father.

9) AGE-DIFF
Age difference between married parents.

10) GET ALONG
How well do your mom and dad get along with each other?

11) CLOSE.MOM
How close do you feel to your mother? (Respondent age 14–17)

12) CLOSE.DAD
How close do you feel to your father? (Respondent age 14–17)

13) ACADEMICS
Teacher's overall rating of student. (Age 12–16)

14) DEGREE
What was the highest grade you completed in school? (Respondent age 17–21)

15) FRIENDS?
Do you feel lonely and wish you had more friends? (Age 12–16)

16) UNHAPPY
How often are you unhappy or sad? (Respondent age 12–16)

17) LOOKS
How do you think your looks compare to other kids your same age? (Respondent age 12–16)

18) AGE.1.DATE
How old were you when you began dating? (Respondent age 17–21)

19) DATE.FREQ
How often do you usually go out on a date? (Respondent age 12–16)

20) DATE.RULES
RULES RE DATING/GOING TO PARTIES (Respondent age 14–17)

21) AGE.1.MEN
At what age did you have your first menstrual period?

22) AGE.1.SEX
How old were you when you had voluntary sexual intercourse for the first time ("18+/not" includes abstainers)

23) BC 1 SEX
Did you use any birth control the first time you had intercourse? (Respondent Age 17–21)

24) FORCED SEX
Was there ever a time when you were forced to have sex against your will, or raped? (Respondent age 12–21)

25) FRNDS SEX?
How many of your friends have had sexual intercourse? (Respondent age 12–16)

26) CH.ATTEND
How often do you attend religious activities? (Respondent age 12–16)

27) NO TROUBLE
I keep out of trouble at all costs. (Respondent age 17–21)

28) ACT QUICK
I often act on the spur of the moment. (Respondent Age 17–21)

29) RUN AWAY?
Before you turned 18 did you ever run away from home? (Respondent age 17–21)

◆ LONG LABEL: STATES ◆

1) STATE NAME

2) SOUTHNESS
DEGREES OF LATITUDE SOUTH OF THE NORTH POLE, BASED ON LOCATION OF STATE CAPITAL. NEW MEX. = COLOR.; ARIZ = UTAH. Omitted cases: Alaska, Hawaii.

3) WESTNESS
DEGREE OF LATITUDE WEST OF PRIME MERIDIAN IS WESTERNMOST POINT OF STATE

4) WARM WINTR
AVERAGE JANUARY LOW TEMPERATURE

5) POP GO 90
1980–90: PERCENT GROWTH (OR DECLINE) IN POPULATION (CENSUS)

6) NO MOVE
1990: PERCENT BORN IN STATE OF RESIDENCE

7) % FOREIGN
1990: PERCENT FOREIGN BORN

8) DENSITY
1990: POPULATION PER SQUARE MILE

9) %URBAN
1990: PERCENT URBAN

10) %RURAL
1990: PERCENT RURAL

11) AVG. AGE
1990: AVERAGE (MEAN) AGE OF THE POPULATION (CENSUS)

12) % UNDER 5
1990: PERCENT OF POPULATION UNDER 5 YEARS

13) % UNDER 18
1990: PERCENT OF POPULATION 17 YEARS OR YOUNGER

14) AGE 5–17
1990: PERCENT OF POPULATION AGE 5–17 (CENSUS)

15) % OVER 65
1990: PERCENT OF POPULATION 65 YEARS OR OLDER

16) % OVER 84
1990: PERCENT OF POPULATION 85 YEARS OR OLDER

17) SEX RATIO
1990: NUMBER OF MALES PER 100 FEMALES

18) %MALE
1990: PERCENT MALE

19) %FEMALE
1990: PERCENT FEMALE

20) % WHITE
1990: PERCENT WHITE

21) % BLACK
1990: PERCENT BLACK

22) % ASIAN
1990: PERCENT ASIAN OR PACIFIC ISLANDERS

23) % HISPANIC
1990: PERCENT OF HISPANIC ORIGIN

24) % NON-ENGL
1990: PERCENT OF THOSE OVER 5 SPEAKING LANGUAGE OTHER THAN ENGLISH
AT HOME

25) %SINGLE
1990: PERCENT OF PERSONS 15 AND OVER WHO HAVE NEVER BEEN MARRIED
(CENSUS)

26) %SINGLE M
1990: PERCENT OF MALES OVER 15 WHO ARE SINGLE

27) %SINGLE F
1990: PERCENT OF FEMALES OVER 15 WHO ARE SINGLE

28) COUPLES
1990: PERCENT OF HOUSEHOLDS WITH MARRIED COUPLES

29) COU.CHLD
1990: PERCENT OF HOUSEHOLDS WITH MARRIED COUPLE WITH OWN CHILDREN

30) COU.NO CH
1990: PERCENT OF HOUSEHOLDS WITH MARRIED COUPLE WITHOUT OWN
CHILDREN

31) BOTH PARNT
1992: PERCENT OF 8TH GRADE STUDENTS WHO REPORT BOTH PARENTS LIVING AT HOME (DES, 1994)

32) %DIVORCED
1990: PERCENT OF THOSE 15 AND OVER WHO CURRENTLY ARE DIVORCED (CENSUS)

33) %M.DIVORCE
1990: PERCENT OF MALES WHO ARE OVER 15 AND DIVORCED

34) %F.DIVORCE
1990: PERCENT OF FEMALES OVER 15 WHO ARE DIVORCED

35) %MALE.HEAD
1990: PERCENT OF HOUSEHOLDS THAT ARE MALE HEADED, NO SPOUSE PRESENT

36) %FEM.HEAD
1990: PERCENT OF HOUSEHOLDS THAT ARE FEMALE HEADED, NO SPOUSE PRESENT

37) ONE P.HH
1990: PERCENT OF HOUSEHOLDS WITH ONE PERSON

38) HHOLD SIZE
1990: PERSONS PER HOUSEHOLD

39) MARRIAGE
1989: MARRIAGES PER 1,000 POPULATION (S.A.,1991)

40) DIVORCE 89
1989: DIVORCES PER 1,000 POPULATION (S.A., 1991)

41) BIRTH
1988: BIRTHS PER 1000 POPULATION (NCHS)

42) TEEN MOMS
1988: PERCENTAGE OF BIRTHS TO MOTHERS UNDER 20 YEARS OLD (NCHS)

43) ADOPTION
1986: NUMBER OF ADOPTIONS PER 100,000 POPULATION (SMAD,1991)

44) ABORTION
1988: ABORTIONS PER 1,000 LIVE BIRTHS (S.A., 1991)

45) MED.FAM $
1989: MEDIAN FAMILY INCOME

46) %POOR.FAM
1989: PERCENT OF FAMILIES BELOW POVERTY LEVEL

47) %NURS.HOME
1990: PERCENT LIVING IN NURSING HOMES

48) NEW HSE $
1990: AVERAGE VALUE OF NEW HOUSING

49) %FEM.WRK90
1990: PERCENT OF FEMALES OVER 16 IN LABOR FORCE

50) AVG TRAVEL
1990: AVERAGE TRAVEL TIME TO WORK FOR THOSE NOT WORKING AT HOME

51) WORK HOME
1990: PERCENT WHO WORK AT HOME

52) DROPOUTS
1990: PERCENT OF PERSONS WHO LEFT SCHOOL WITHOUT GRADUATING FROM
HIGH SCHOOL (WA, 1993)

53) % COLLEGE
1990: PERCENT OF THOSE 25 OR OVER WHO HAVE COMPLETED A COLLEGE
DEGREE (BACHELOR'S, GRADUATE, OR PROFESSIONAL DEGREE)

54) PUPIL/TCH
1992: PUPIL/TEACHER RATIO (DES,1994)

55) $PER PUPIL
1991: EXPENDITURES (IN DOLLARS) PER PUPIL IN PUBLIC ELEMENTARY AND SEC-
ONDARY SCHOOLS (S.R., 1992)

56) TEACHER$
1992–1993: AVERAGE TEACHER'S SALARY (DES, 1994)

57) MATH SCORE
1991: AVERAGE MATH PROFICIENCY SCORES BY 8TH GRADERS (USA TODAY:6/7/91)

58) VERBAL SAT
1992: VERBAL SCORE ON SAT (DES, 1994)

59) MATH SAT
1992: MATHEMATICAL SCORE ON SAT (DES, 1994)

60) %TAK.SAT
1992: PERCENT OF GRADUATES TAKING THE SAT (DES, 1994)

61) CH.MEMBER
1990: PERCENT OF POPULATION BELONGING TO A LOCAL CHURCH (CHURCH)

62) %NO RELIG
1990: PERCENT OF THE POPULATION WHO SAY THEY HAVE NO RELIGION
(KOSMIN)

63) % CATHOLIC
1990: PERCENT OF THE POPULATION WHO GIVE THEIR RELIGIOUS PREFERENCE
AS CATHOLIC (KOSMIN)

64) % BAPTIST
1990: PERCENT OF THE POPULATION WHO GIVE THEIR RELIGIOUS PREFERENCE
AS BAPTIST (KOSMIN)

65) SUICIDE
1989: SUICIDES PER 100,000 (MVSR 1/7/92)

66) COKE USERS
1990: COCAINE ADDICTS PER 1,000 POPULATION (SENATE JUDICIARY COMMITTEE, USA TODAY: 8/6/90)

67) P.CRIME
1990: PROPERTY CRIMES PER 100,000 (UCR, 1991)

68) V.CRIME
1990: VIOLENT CRIMES PER 100,000 (UCR, 1991)

69) RAPE
1990: FORCIBLE RAPES PER 100,000 (UCR, 1991)

70) BEER
1989: GALLONS OF BEER CONSUMED PER PERSON 16 AND OVER (HCSR, 1993)

71) WINE
1989: GALLONS OF WINE CONSUMED PER PERSON 16 AND OVER (HCSR, 1993)

72) SYPHILIS
1991: REPORTED CASES OF SYPHILIS PER 100,000 (MMWR, 1/3/92)

73) AIDS
1991: TOTAL NUMBER OF AIDS DEATHS PER 100,000 THROUGH 1991 (HEALTH, 1992)

74) %CLINTON92
1992: PERCENT OF VOTES FOR CLINTON (DEM.) (WA, 1993)

75) MDs
1990: NUMBER OF PHYSICIANS (M.D.s) PER 100,000 (HCSR, 1993)

76) SHRINKS
1990: NUMBER OF PSYCHIATRISTS PER 100,000 (HCSR, 1993)

77) %FEM MD
1990: PERCENT OF PHYSICIANS (M.D.s) WHO ARE FEMALE (HCSR, 1993)

78) %FEM VET
1990: PERCENT OF FEMALES WHO ARE VETERANS

79) VIET VETS
1990: PERCENT OF VETERANS FROM VIETNAM ERA

80) %LEGION
1983: PERCENT OF MILITARY VETERANS WHO BELONG TO THE AMERICAN LEGION (AMERICAN LEGION)

81) TV>6HRS
1992: PERCENT OF 8TH GRADE STUDENTS WHO REPORT WATCHING 6 OR MORE HOURS OF TELEVISION EACH DAY (DES, 1994)

82) TV DISH
1990: SATELLITE TV DISHES PER 10,000 (ORBIT MAG. 3/1991)

83) PLAYBOY
1990: PLAYBOY CIRCULATION PER 100,000 POPULATION (ABC)

84) FLD&STREAM
1990: CIRCULATION OF FIELD & STREAM MAGAZINE PER 100,000 (ABC)

85) PET$PER
1982: RETAIL SALES BY PET STORES PER CAPITA, IN DOLLARS (RETAIL)

86) MS.
1983: CIRCULATION OF MS. MAGAZINE PER 1000 POPULATION (ABC)

87) LIBRARY
1989: PUBLIC LIBRARIES (AND BRANCHES) PER 10,000 (S.R.,1992)

88) BOOK $ PER
1987: PER CAPITA RETAIL SALES BY BOOKSTORES (RETAIL)

89) HUNTING
1990: NUMBER OF RESIDENTS WHO PURCHASED HUNTING LICENSES PER 1,000
POPULATION (U.S.FISH & WILDLIFE)

90) FISHING
1990: NUMBER OF RESIDENTS WHO PURCHASED FISHING LICENSES PER 1,000
(U.S.FISH & WILDLIFE)

91) %FEM.WRK40
1940: PERCENT OF FEMALES OVER 14 IN THE LABOR FORCE

92) MEDIAN$ 40
1940: MEDIAN ANNUAL WAGE OR SALARY INCOME (IN DOLLARS)

93) MARRIAGE40
1940: MARRIAGES PER 1000 POPULATION: NEVADA (354) TREATED AS MISSING DTA

94) F WAGES 20
1920: AVERAGE MONTHLY PAY (WITHOUT BOARD) FOR A FARM HAND IN $

95) %FEM.WRK20
1920: % FEMALES 16 AND OVER IN LABOR FORCE

96) DIVORCE 22
1922: DIVORCES PER 1000 POPULATION Omitted case: Nevada = 13.25

LICENSE AGREEMENT

READ THIS LICENSE AGREEMENT CAREFULLY BEFORE OPENING THE DISKETTE PACKAGE. BY OPENING THIS PACKAGE YOU ACCEPT THE TERMS OF THIS AGREEMENT. *MicroCase*® Corporation, hereinafter called the Licensor, grants the purchaser of this software, hereinafter called the Licensee, the right to use and reproduce the following software: **Marriage and Family:** *An Introduction Using MicroCase* in accordance with the following terms and conditions.

Permitted Uses

◆ You may use this software only for educational purposes.

◆ You may use the software on any compatible computer, provided the software is used on only one computer and by one user at a time.

◆ You may make a backup copy of the diskette(s).

Prohibited Uses

◆ You may not use this software for any purposes other than educational purposes.

◆ You may not make copies of the documentation or program disk, except backup copies as described above.

◆ You may not distribute, rent, sub-license or lease the software or documentation.

◆ You may not alter, modify, or adapt the software or documentation, including, but not limited to, translating, decompiling, disassembling, or creating derivative works.

◆ You may not use the software on a network, file server, or virtual disk.

THIS AGREEMENT IS EFFECTIVE UNTIL TERMINATED. IT WILL TERMINATE IF LICENSEE FAILS TO COMPLY WITH ANY TERM OR CONDITION OF THIS AGREEMENT. LICENSEE MAY TERMINATE IT AT ANY OTHER TIME BY DESTROYING THE SOFTWARE TOGETHER WITH ALL COPIES. IF THIS AGREEMENT IS TERMINATED BY LICENSOR, LICENSEE AGREES TO EITHER DESTROY OR RETURN THE ORIGINAL AND ALL EXISTING COPIES OF THE SOFTWARE TO THE LICENSOR WITHIN FIVE (5) DAYS AFTER RECEIVING NOTICE OF TERMINATION FROM THE LICENSOR.

MicroCase Corporation retains all rights not expressly granted in this License Agreement. Nothing in the License Agreement constitutes a waiver of MicroCase Corporation's rights under the U.S. copyright laws or any other Federal or State Law.

Should you have any questions concerning this Agreement, you may contact MicroCase Corporation by writing to: MicroCase Corporation, 1301 120th Avenue N.E., Bellevue, WA 98005, ATTN: College Publishing Division.